Perspectives on School Mathematics

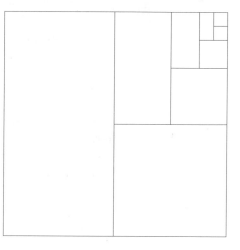

Measuring Up

Prototypes for Mathematics Assessment

Mathematical Sciences Education Board
National Research Council

NATIONAL ACADEMY PRESS
Washington, DC   1993

NATIONAL ACADEMY PRESS
2101 Constitution Avenue, NW • Washington, DC 20418

NOTICE: The project that is the subject of this report was approved by the Governing Board of the National Research Council, whose members are drawn from the councils of the National Academy of Sciences, the National Academy of Engineering, and the Institute of Medicine. The members of the committee responsible for the report were chosen for their special competences and with regard for appropriate balance.

This report has been reviewed by a group other than the authors according to procedures approved by a Report Review Committee consisting of members of the National Academy of Sciences, the National Academy of Engineering, and the Institute of Medicine.

The National Research Council was organized by the National Academy of Sciences in 1916 to associate the broad community of science and technology with the Academy's purposes of furthering knowledge and advising the federal government. Functioning in accordance with general policies determined by the Academy, the Council has become the principal operating agency of both the National Academy of Sciences and the National Academy of Engineering in providing services to the government, the public, and the scientific and engineering communities. The Council is administered jointly by both Academies and the Institute of Medicine. Dr. Frank Press and Dr. Robert M. White are chairman and vice chairman, respectively, of the National Research Council.

The Mathematical Sciences Education Board was established in 1985 to provide a continuing national overview and assessment capability for mathematics education and is concerned with excellence in mathematical sciences education for all students at all levels. The Board reports directly to the Governing Board of the National Research Council.

Library of Congress Catalog Card Number 92-62904
International Standard Book Number 0-309-04845-1

Printed in the United States of America

B081

BK # 10.95

Preface

As the United States moves resolutely towards standards-based education, we must learn anew how to measure quality — of students' learning, of teachers' performance, of school and district accomplishment. Assessment demonstrates the real meaning of "standards." We can see in the tasks children are expected to perform just what they must learn to meet our national goals.

It is all too clear that current tests used for assessment of educational performance fail to measure adequately progress toward national standards. This is especially true in mathematics, where curriculum and teaching standards recommended by the National Council of Teachers of Mathematics have earned nationwide consensus. Yet commonly used tests continue to stress routine, repetitive, rote tasks instead of offering children opportunities to demonstrate the full range of their mathematical power, including such important facets as communication, problem solving, inventiveness, persistence, and curiosity. In *Measuring Up*, the National Research Council seeks to demonstrate in one specific instance — fourth grade mathematics — one approach to standards-based assessment.

The prototypes in this volume are intended to bring the ethos of the standards to life in concrete assessment tasks. A superficial glance at the tasks will convince any reader that the new mathematics standards call for a significantly different type of education. But these prototypes do more than illustrate standards. They contribute to a public debate on significant redirection of U.S. traditions concerning the role of assessment in education, including these key issues:

- Should assessments set goals for learning, or merely sample the present curriculum? Typically, nations that routinely outperform the United States in international comparisons link assessment to goals for learning, and make both goals and assessments known in advance to parents, teachers, students, and the public. In the United States, in contrast, our standardized tests are largely hidden from public view and measure only a very limited part of school curricula.

- Should assessments tell us what students cannot do or what each student can do? The new standards stress broad and flexible approaches to problem solving, making use of many different approaches and mathematical tools. Yet most tests continue to emphasize set questions with a limited number of options for student responses and rarely provide sufficient flexibility for students to display the full range of their knowledge or abilities.

- Should students be judged only on their individual work, or also on their ability to work together for the benefit of a larger group? Both in business and in society, real problem solving requires individuals to work together. The new standards for mathematics education stress communication, cooperation, and group performance as an important component of mathematical power. Yet traditional testing in the United States measures only the individual, elevating competition over cooperation as if education were a zero-sum game.

- How can assessment encourage and recognize inventive, imaginative responses that, although unexpected, are constructive and appropriate? In traditional testing, the examiner determines what topic an item is "intended" to measure. But in assessment attuned to the holistic nature of the new standards, as are the prototypes in this volume, the measure of students' responses is not so much how well they anticipate what the examiner had in mind, but how well they apply their own minds to the task at hand.

As our nation needs standards in curriculum and teaching, so too we need standards for assessment. Without such standards, we will continue, unwisely, to measure what is convenient rather than what is most important. In 1991 the Mathematical Sciences Education Board called attention to the need for new thinking about assessment through a National Summit on Assessment. The National Council of Teachers of Mathematics is now working, in cooperation with the MSEB, to develop needed standards for assessment.

Our nation's drive towards standards-based education will not be complete until joined with appropriate assessment. *Measuring Up* is an important step in the process of encouraging widespread debate about the long-term direction of assessment in U.S. education.

Frank Press, *Chairman*
National Research Council

Foreword

The mathematics assessment prototypes in this document were developed by a writing group consisting of the following individuals: Lowell Carmony (Lake Forest College); Robert Davis (Rutgers University); Susan Jo Russell (TERC); Joan Rutherford (Haynesbridge, Georgia Public Schools); Lourdes Santiago (Boston Public Schools); and Paul Shoecraft (University of Houston at Victoria). The group began its work in the summer of 1991 and was involved in pilot testing of tasks throughout the project. On behalf of the MSEB, I want to thank each member of the writing group for his or her thoughtful contributions to this challenging task.

The tasks themselves, without the surrounding explanatory materials, were read by a number of people with long-standing interest in mathematics assessment: Philip Daro (California Mathematics Project); Bonnie Hole (Princeton Institute for Research); Roberta Flexer (University of Colorado at Boulder); Jo Ann Mosier (Kentucky State Department of Education); Thomas Romberg (University of Wisconsin at Madison); Joel Schneider (Children's Television Workshop); and Jean Kerr Stenmark (Lawrence Hall of Science). We are grateful for their many thoughtful comments and insight. Nonetheless, the tasks that appear in this manuscript are the responsibility of the MSEB and do not necessarily reflect the position or views of these readers.

We thank the many people who were involved in the pilot testing of the prototypes at various stages of the project: Alice Alston, Amy Boyd, Pam Brown, Vanessa Burns, Deanna Callahan, Lowell Carmony, Robert Davis, Doris Ann Edwards, Lisa Johnson, Carolyn Maher, Suzanne Rogers, Mary Russ, and

Paul Shoecraft. We are also grateful to the principals, mathematics supervisors, and teachers associated with the trial classrooms, for allowing the pilot testing to interrupt their normal activities.

Financial support for the project was provided by the National Research Council and the National Science Foundation. Additionally, the New Standards Project assisted with the first meeting of the Writing Group, which was held concurrently with a New Standards Project meeting in Snowmass, Colorado. We gratefully acknowledge the support of these organizations.

We owe a special thanks to Edward Esty, who managed endless details of this complex project with patience and wisdom, and to Linda P. Rosen, who coordinated the overall effort as staff officer for the project.

Finally, we thank the students who worked on these tasks. The written work of some of them appears as examples in this volume, and all of them provided invaluable feedback.

Lynn A Steen

Lynn Arthur Steen, *Executive Director*
Mathematical Sciences Education Board

Contents

Introduction

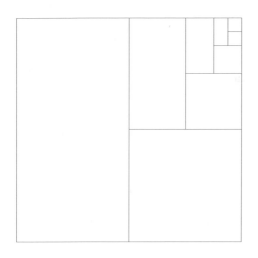

Goals for School Mathematics

The 1989 NCTM report *Curriculum and Evaluation Standards for School Mathematics* identifies five broad goals for students' study of mathematics:

- *To value mathematics.* Students must recognize the varied roles played by mathematics in society, from accounting and finance to scientific research, from public policy debates to market research and political polls. Students' experiences in school must bring them to believe that mathematics has value for them, so they will have the incentive to continue studying mathematics as long as they are in school.

- *To reason mathematically.* Mathematics is, above all else, a habit of mind that helps clarify complex situations. Students must learn to gather evidence, to make conjectures, to formulate models, to invent counterexamples, and to build sound arguments. In so doing, they will develop the informed skepticism and sharp insight for which the mathematical perspective is so valued by society.

- *To communicate mathematics.* Learning to read, to write, and to speak about mathematical topics is essential not only as an objective in itself — in order that knowledge learned can be effectively used — but also as a strategy for understanding. There are no better ways to learn mathematics than by working in groups, teaching mathematics to each other, arguing about strategies, and expressing arguments carefully in written form.

- *To solve problems.* Industry expects school graduates to be able to use a wide variety of mathematical methods to solve problems. Students must, therefore, experience a wide variety of problems that vary in context, in length, in difficulty, and in method. They must learn to recast vague problems in a form amenable to analysis; to select appropriate strategies for solving problems; to recognize and formulate several solutions when that is appropriate; and to work with others in reaching consensus on solutions that are effective as well as logical.

- *To develop confidence.* The ability of individuals to cope with the mathematical demands of everyday life — as employees, as parents, and as citizens — depends on the attitudes toward mathematics conveyed by school experiences. One of the paradoxes of our age is the spectacle of parents who recognize the importance of mathematics yet boast of their own mathematical incompetence. Mathematics can neither be learned nor used unless it is supported by self-confidence built on success.

Measuring What's Worth Learning

The spotlight of educational reform continues to sweep across the stage of mathematics. First curriculum, then teaching, and now assessment have come under intense professional and public scrutiny. Amid deteriorating public confidence in the quality of American education, the mathematical community is addressing multiple challenges to articulate and implement effective standards in the key arena of testing, assessment, and accountability.

In the center of the assessment stage are three elements contesting for leadership. Conventional testing offers comfortable short-response tests on traditional content that are taken by millions of students every year. Reformers, including authors of the two K-12 *Standards* documents from the National Council of Teachers of Mathematics (NCTM), call for fundamental change — different in content, in format, and particularly in spirit. To this well-rehearsed contest of traditionalist vs. reformist has now been added a third movement arriving from outside the educational community: the political call for assessment of progress towards our nation's new standards in mathematics education.

In the decade since publication of *A Nation at Risk,* the United States has moved a long way toward a new consensus for education. Talk of national standards, once taboo, is now commonplace; so too is talk of alternative school structures and innovative licensure for teachers. It is now time to develop a new national understanding of standards-based performance as the true measure of educational progress.

Throughout this decade, mathematics has led the way in educational reform. The 1989 MSEB publication *Everybody Counts* was followed in just two months by publication of the NCTM *Curriculum and Evaluation Standards for School Mathematics,* with its theme of developing mathematical power in all students. Undergirding these reports are three fundamental principles of testing, assessment, and accountability:

- Tests should measure what's worth learning, not just what's easy to measure.

- Progress depends on constant correction based on feedback from assessment.

- Schools are accountable, both to taxpayers and to students.

Even as the renewed public scrutiny compels educators to demonstrate that children are learning, the NCTM's *Standards* require new ways of measuring what is being learned. Because the linkage between tests and teaching is so close, it is vitally important for the United States that assessment be based on instruments that are properly aligned with the goals of the *Standards.*

The Challenge

At the National Summit on Mathematics Assessment in April 1991, Governor Roy Romer, in his capacity as Co-chair of the National Education Goals Panel, challenged the mathematical community to show the nation what mathematics educators mean by mathematical power and what new and more demanding standards will mean for our young people. One month later, the MSEB authorized creation of *prototypes* of tasks that could be used to assess fourth-graders' mathematical skills and knowledge, thereby providing examples of what children

Why we are doing this

educated according to the new standards should be able to do. They wanted to be sure that the voice of mathematics was heard early and clearly in the assessment reform movement. The MSEB determined that it should be prepared to show, by example, the type of assessment exercises that would be appropriate to measure our nation's progress toward the goals of mathematics education.

To create the prototypes, the MSEB subsequently convened a small writing group of mathematics educators, teachers, and mathematicians. Taking up Governor Romer's challenge, the writing group created a sampler of tasks to encompass many of the goals for mathematics instruction that are expressed in the NCTM *Standards.* These tasks, which illustrate what a standards-based education really means, have been pilot tested on a limited basis in four states. Many have been revised, often more than once, but all can benefit from continued improvement and adaptations.

Readers who skip ahead will see that these prototypes are not only innovative and challenging but also just plain fun. Teachers, children, and even parents should find these tasks both engaging and surprising. We invite readers to try them, either before or after reading the surrounding analysis.

The Criteria

Not surprisingly, the MSEB writing group debated extensively the criteria for prototypical assessment tasks. They faced the pioneer's challenge — to use incomplete information as a basis for decisions whose consequences are difficult to foresee. From these discussions emerged several criteria that helped shape the nature and selection of prototypes in this volume:

What we are trying to do

- *Mathematical content:* The tasks should reflect the "spirit" of the reform movement, but not necessarily be limited by particular curricular content, present or planned. Many of the tasks should incorporate a variety of mathematics, particularly in areas such as statistics, geometry, and probability that are least often emphasized in traditional K-4 programs.

- *Mathematical connections:* Everyone involved in the mathematics reform movement, from classroom teach-

ers to national policy makers, agrees on the importance
of connecting mathematics — to science, to social science, to art, to everyday life, and to other parts of mathematics. Accordingly, the prototypes should develop
links with science, with the visual arts, and with the
language arts.

- *Thoughtful approaches:* Insofar as possible, the tasks
  should promote "higher-order" thinking. Just as the
  verbs explore, justify, represent, solve, construct, discuss, use, investigate, describe, develop, and predict
  are used in the *Standards* to convey "active physical
  and mental involvement of children" in learning mathematics, they are appropriate to seek in assessment
  activities as well. Further, given a choice between cog-
  nitive complexity and simplicity, the focus of these
  tasks should be on the former.

- *Mathematical communication:* The tasks should
  emphasize the importance of communicating results —
  not simply isolated answers, but mathematical representations and chains of reasoning. Children should have
  opportunities to work in groups to explain their thinking
  to others, and to write explanations of their approaches.

- *Rich opportunities:* The tasks should let children solve
  problems via a variety of creative strategies; demonstrate talents (artistic, spatial, verbal) beyond those nor-
  mally associated with numerical mathematics; invent
  mathematics that (to them) is new; recognize opportunities to use and apply mathematics; and show what
  they can do (as opposed to what they cannot do).

- *Improved instruction:* The tasks should have the potential for influencing instruction positively, both in content and in pedagogy. Teachers who use these tasks
  should become better teachers as a result of the experience; children who participate should emerge with
  increased self-confidence and heightened expectations
  for future mathematics courses.

The Caveats

These tasks are *prototypes,* not tasks ready for immediate administration to fourth-grade students. They are intended to illustrate possible directions for new assessment instruments, not to be an example of a real assessment. Certainly they should be viewed as work in progress, not as fully completed blueprints.

Criteria related to cost, efficiency, and immediate feasibility were deliberately not imposed on the work of the writing group. These are important considerations for implementation, but not for this volume. The MSEB goal for *Measuring Up* is to promote long-term change, not to write assessment material for current courses.

As assessment instruments, these prototypes are intended for children who have had the full benefit of a *Standards*-caliber mathematical education in kindergarten through fourth grade. Hence the tasks as presented here will be more appropriate, generally speaking, for students of some time in the future. From the perspective that has historically dominated U.S. testing, these prototypes illustrate directions for tomorrow, rather than tasks for immediate practical use.

> *What we are not trying to do*

From a perspective more common in Europe — where tests, appropriately publicized in advance, set targets for teaching and learning — these prototypes do serve the immediate purpose of defining appropriate goals for fourth-grade instruction.

Moreover, the prototypes, as a set, are not intended to illustrate a single assessment that treats all of the mathematics important at the fourth-grade level. Much that is important in the curriculum is not covered adequately in the particular examples chosen for this volume. Nevertheless, to expand our view of appropriate mathematics goals for the primary grades, these tasks provide more opportunities for children to demonstrate their ideas in areas often missing from the curriculum (e.g., data, geometry) than in areas already well entrenched (arithmetic). The imbalance in these examples reflects our desire to illustrate the new, not an effort to reshape the curriculum to fit this particular set of examples.

These prototypes, which are tasks to be done in time spans ranging from one to three class periods, represent only one of many important forms of assessment. Other forms of assessment are essential for a balanced program, including *projects* (extended pieces of mathematical investigation designed to take a substantial block of time), *portfolios* (structured collections of student work gathered over a long time period), and *tests* (time-limited responses to shorter tasks). Some of the references at the end of this volume (e.g., Pandey [1991]; Stenmark [1989]) describe these alternative approaches.

The Audience

Many readers of *Measuring Up* will be persons who are professionally concerned with mathematics education, particularly developers of tests and other assessment instruments. For such

Whom we are trying to reach

people, both those who work within commercial test development companies as well as those in educational settings at the state or local levels, *Measuring Up* should stimulate development of new approaches to assessment that reflect the broad goals of the nation's standards for mathematics education.

If mandated assessments evolve to resemble more closely the ones suggested in this book, it is clear that different approaches to instruction and testing will be needed. Hence school administrators and educational policy makers will also be affected by the changes implicit in these prototypes. The tasks will convey to the audience of policy makers and education leaders what mathematics educators mean by assessment reform.

A third audience for *Measuring Up* consists of classroom teachers, and not just those at the fourth-grade level. It is only natural that many practicing elementary school teachers may find some of these tasks to be somewhat daunting, especially if their students have not had the mathematical preparation that the tasks assume. Teachers should look at the prototypes not as current expectations, but rather as goals to aim for. The prototypes can be viewed both as examples of what tomorrow's assessment in mathematics might be like, and as examples of what today's goals for instruction should be like. In the meantime, teachers can use them as ideas for instructional activities for today. (A list of resources for teachers including the names and addresses of contacts in each state appears at the end of the volume.)

Another audience is the community of university-based educators who are responsible for the pre-service education of prospective teachers. They will find *Measuring Up* to be a source of ideas to use today for connecting the tenets of the mathematics education reform movement to classroom practice.

Finally, of course, the ultimate audience for these new assessment tasks and the ideas that underlie them is the elementary school children for whom the tasks were designed. The tasks provide good examples of challenging mathematical problems and situations that effective teachers can use even now as part of their instructional strategies. Today's children can begin to see the challenge in authentic mathematical problems even before tomorrow's tests give them an opportunity to demonstrate their accomplishments.

The Prototypes

Measuring Up contains thirteen assessment prototypes that exemplify changes called for in the *Standards.* In some cases the particular settings or contexts for the tasks are original, while in other cases some aspect of the task has appeared in another form previously.

The tasks in *Measuring Up* are intended for a largely hypothetical audience: fourth-grade children who have had a K-4 mathematics experience fully consonant with the NCTM *Standards.* Unfortunately, very few U.S. fourth graders have had the benefit of such an education. This is, of course, the whole point of the reform effort. One

What we have accomplished

would not expect many of today's fourth graders to do very well on these tasks. Nonetheless the aim was to keep the tasks *accessible* to most of today's fourth graders; they should at least be able to understand what the tasks are about and become engaged in working on them.

Too often test questions and assessment tasks are presented solely in written form, which may be a burden for poor readers and for children whose first language is not English. Such children might not be able to respond to the tasks in a way that shows their true level of mathematical knowledge or skills. Many alternative presentations are possible: videotaped introduction; teacher-taught introduction; computer-based presentation; and presentation using manipulative materials. The prototypes illustrate each of these alternative modes of presentation, and two of the tasks are written in Spanish as well as in English.

Notwithstanding the possible variety in presentation, the prototypes in *Measuring Up* adhere to a certain uniformity of structure. Most are organized as a sequence of questions, often of increasing difficulty. On the one hand, this provides a structure around which the child's problem solving must be organized. On the other hand, this sequence of questions may suggest that the problem-poser, rather than the problem-solver, is in charge of the problem-solving process. Although other forms of organization are certainly possible, these prototypes provide sufficient imposed structure to help the mathematically less sophisticated student get started and show what he or she can do, while allowing plenty of open-ended space at the top to challenge the more advanced student. Even though the questions within a task often grow in difficulty, many of the tasks involve problem solving, reasoning, and communication right from the beginning. These are important aspects of mathematics for all children.

Just as the tasks are presented in several formats, so they are also designed to give children a chance to respond in a variety of modes — perhaps by constructing an object or by creating a pattern on a computer screen. One important response mode that is not specifically included in these prototypes is that of the child talking individually to a teacher, explaining his or her solutions orally rather than in written form. Pilot testing of the tasks has shown that children who have not had considerable experience in organizing their thoughts on paper find it much easier to tell someone else what they are doing than it is to record it in writing. Teachers who use tasks like the ones in this collection for their own informal assessment of how children are progressing mathematically will want to supplement written responses with spoken ones. In fact, asking a child to explain a solution in two forms — spoken and written — can help the child to sharpen and deepen both responses.

These prototypes can be used either for informal classroom-based assessment by an individual teacher, or for more formal external assessment, although certain modifications may be necessary to make the tasks suitable for a given purpose. All of the prototypes call for responses that go well beyond simple numerical answers, and most require the student to explain underlying patterns, relationships, or reasoning. As a result, the same activities can be useful to an individual teacher as she or he tries to discern more deeply how students are progressing mathematically, and to a district to discern the effectiveness of its instruction.

As the NCTM *Standards* urge, assessment should be embedded in instruction, so that most children would not recognize the assessment activity as a "test." Even when certain tasks are used as part of a formal, external assessment, there should be some kind of instructional follow-up. As a routine part of classroom discourse, interesting problems should be revisited, extended, and generalized, whatever their original sources.

Increasingly, educators are recognizing the value of having children work together in groups. Certainly group work exemplifies the NCTM's goal of stressing mathematics as a means of communication. Some of the tasks in *Measuring Up* are designed to be carried out in small groups, while in other cases, small groups are certainly a reasonable option. Continuing experimentation will be required to determine how the children can best be grouped for assessment tasks like these, and how to weigh individual vs. group work in performance evaluation.

In several cases the problems suggested here for fourth grade could also be asked in the eighth or even the twelfth grade, although naturally the expected sophistication and completeness of the responses would be very different. If a mathematical task is genuinely interesting and worthwhile for fourth graders, there is no reason why it should not be worthwhile for older children, or even for adults.

The Tryouts

Each prototype was tested on several score fourth-grade students in a number of different locales. These "tryouts" were not designed to be either representative or comprehensive, but to aid in improving the tasks. This they did, but they did much more as well. By observing how students react to the prototypes, we learned much about the gulf

What we learned from children

that separates current students from the goals of the *Standards*. We also learned that we are novices on how these new forms of assessment will work in the classroom.

Three examples can illustrate the types of surprises that all teachers will encounter as they begin to explore and extend these prototypes:

- In a few cases the tasks as originally presented seemed not to be sufficiently challenging. One example is the "Lightning" task in which a fairly large proportion of the students could easily handle the map-reading requirements. So a question dealing with locating a lightning bolt that is a given distance from two observers was added.

- Sometimes a proposed task yielded no information of any interest at all. In "Bridges," there was originally a more open-ended question in which students were to create their own bridges. Nobody created anything that went even a little bit beyond the two-support, single-span examples. This may have been due to the wording of the question, to the backgrounds of the particular students, or to some other factor. This lack of inventiveness and perseverance is something worth pursuing since creativity is an essential part of doing mathematics, for fourth graders as well as for everyone else. However, since the question produced virtually no information, it was dropped.

- One whole prototype was dropped entirely. It was a task on what is known as "Pick's Theorem" — which relates the area of a polygonal region on a geoboard to the number of nails on the boundary and in the interior of the region. The task was extremely open-ended and required extensive interaction between the teacher and individual students or small groups of students. Even if one assumed (as we do) that the teachers involved in the assessment are uniformly well versed in the subtleties of the underlying mathematics, there seemed to be no way of separating the effects of the teacher from the progress that individual students might make on the task. Perhaps such a task could be viewed as an assessment of the teacher-class unit, but in any case it seemed to be too problematic to include in this collection.

The Format

Each of the thirteen tasks is presented using the same outline. After the title, there is a suggested *time allotment,* which can vary from one to three class periods. This is followed by a suggested *student social organization,* although in many cases the task does not depend substantively on a particular form of grouping.

Next comes the task itself. First there is a description of *assumed background.* In most cases this refers to specific aspects of the children's mathematical background, assuming — hypothetically, of course — that the children have had a K-4 education that fully meets the

How we present the prototypes

NCTM *Standards.* Second, there is a section on *presenting the task,* which details exactly what the teacher (or other assessor) should do. Finally, there is the *student assessment activity.* Very often this involves one or more sheets of paper on which students record their responses. (To reproduce these pages, which were scaled to the 7" x 10" page of this volume, the copying machine should be set to magnify them appropriately.)

The next major section is a *rationale* for the mathematics education community, which in many respects is the heart of *Measuring Up*. This is where comments on the content, style, or intent of the task appear (e.g., why the task was included), as well as more general messages about mathematics education that the task is intended to convey.

Following the main presentation of the rationale for the task, there are two subsections that provide further information. The first, task design considerations, discusses some of the details behind the task — why certain questions were phrased as they were, or why particular numbers were chosen. The second, variants and extensions, hints at other directions in which the task could be taken, for purposes either of instruction or further assessment. These subsections are far from exhaustive, for often the tasks could be starting points for weeks of instruction. One important message conveyed by this section is that these particular prototypes are in no way unique.

The next section describes a rough scoring system — what is called a *protorubric* — for the task. It is now widely recognized that an assessment task by itself means little without an indication of how children's responses would be scored. In other words, an important component of an assessment task is a scoring rubric that describes and orders a variety of answers that a child might typically give. For reasons discussed in the next section, the rubrics given here are necessarily tentative and incomplete — whence "protorubrics."

Finally, in some of the tasks there is a section containing *references* to relevant sources.

The Protorubrics

Although each task in this volume contains commentary about scoring based on student work, for a number of reasons we have not developed fully detailed scoring rubrics:

How might fourth graders do?

- The intended audience for these tasks are students who have had a mathematical education that is different from what is commonly available in U.S. schools today.

Ideally, a scoring rubric should be based on the responses of many hundreds of children who are properly prepared for the tasks. While all of these tasks have been pilot tested with children, in most cases the testing has not been sufficient to provide a solid base for a complete scoring rubric.

- There is no universal agreement on how to structure scoring rubrics. Various groups who are currently active in creating alternative assessments in mathematics have used different styles and different levels of specificity (for example, four vs. six levels of gradation) for scoring rubrics.

- A complete analysis of scoring rubrics would require a foray into the thorny problem of judging individual performance in group settings. Although we do intend that these prototypes will encourage teachers to use group work, we have deliberately set aside the daunting task of codifying rubrics for assigning individual grades when students work in groups.

- There is continuing debate between proponents of "holistic" and "analytic" approaches. Does one look at every isolated component of a complex response, or should one make a general, overall, judgment of the child's response? While it is important to be fairly specific about what the task is intended to elicit and about what is to be valued in children's responses, there is no compelling evidence to favor one position over the other. The protorubrics given in this book can easily be adapted to different styles.

Moreover, protorubrics are in some ways analogous to standards: they express goals, ensure quality, and promote change in assessment. Hence, protorubrics by themselves may have a unique contribution to make to assessment reform, whether or not they ever are formalized into polished rubrics.

The protorubrics in *Measuring Up* are structured around three levels: high, medium, and low. Rather than try to define precisely what constitutes a "high" response, the protorubrics list only selected characteristics of a high response. We leave to others the additional steps required to turn these outlines into fully detailed scoring rubrics and to refine the levels of response to each task.

One important purpose of creating a scoring rubric is to communicate to the *students* exactly what is expected of them. Embedded in our assumption that the students have had an exemplary mathematics education is an implication that appropriate standards have already been communicated to the students. Thus, for example, when a protorubric mentions a "clear explanation" or an "appropriate drawing," it is assumed that the children and the assessor share a common understanding of what these terms mean.

Another purpose to is to help the *teacher* interpret students' responses by specifying or clarifying the mathematical essence of the task — which aspects of the task are critical mathematically and which are not. These clarifications will be improved as tasks such as these are tested with larger numbers of students, particularly with those who have studied in a *Standards*-based curriculum.

The Standards

Since this entire project has been undertaken in a context of mathematics education reform, an important question that naturally arises is the extent

Are we measuring the right things?

to which these prototypes reflect the spirit of the NCTM's *Curriculum and Evaluation Standards for School Mathematics.* Figure 1 suggests how these particular tasks relate to the content that the *Standards* calls for in grades K-4.

Having constructed this figure, we must emphasize how potentially dangerous such tables can be because they promote a "check-off" approach that conflicts with a truly integrated view of mathematics. Each "x" within the body of the table is merely shorthand for a detailed account of how the particular task exemplifies, or illustrates, or even extends the ideas within that particular standard.

In some cases, the "x" means only that the idea is possibly, but not necessarily, involved in the task. For example, an "x" appears in the intersection of the "Hog Game" task and Fractions and Decimals because, as the protorubric states, one effective approach to the question about competing strategies depends on calculating each player's expected score, and this will require work with fractions or decimals. Similarly, children might create fractions to knock down pins in the "Bowl-A-Fact" task, and fractions could arise as part of finding an average number of buttons per person in "How Many Buttons?" Indeed, any sufficiently rich mathematical problem will allow for a variety of different approaches, and so the mathematics actually used may vary from one student to another. (On the surface, this appears to pose

yet more difficulties for grading and judgment since student responses may be entirely satisfactory even while ignoring the skills supposedly being examined. Taking the broader view, however, the aim in these prototypes is to assess mathematical power, not individual specific skills.)

It is clear from the chart that the tasks have been designed so that each of them touches several of the NCTM *Standards*. (Note in particular that every task involves the four all-pervasive standards of problem-solving, communication, reasoning, and connections.) Of course it is a deliberate goal of these particular tasks to emphasize that mathematics is a connected and coherent discipline. Assessment tasks designed to involve many areas within mathematics will promote the parallel idea that instructional activities should also cross boundaries between topics.

Figure 1 also shows how the tasks are arrayed with respect to some aspects of mathematics that go beyond the NCTM *Standards* for K-4. Two of these — discrete mathematics and algebra — appear as components of standards in higher grades. Drawing attention to them here is meant only to suggest that

Figure 1 NCTM *Standards* and Prototypes of Fourth-Grade Assessment Tasks

K-4 Standards	Mystery Graphs	Checkers Tournament	Bridges	Hexarights	Bowl-A-Fact	Point of View	Quilt Designer	How Many Buttons?	Taxman	Lightning	Bears	Towers	Hog Game
1. Problem Solving	X	X	X	X	X	X	X	X	X	X	X	X	X
2. Mathematics as Communication	X	X	X	X	X	X	X	X	X	X	X	X	X
3. Mathematics as Reasoning	X	X	X	X	X	X	X	X	X	X	X	X	X
4. Mathematical Connections	X	X	X	X	X	X	X	X	X	X	X	X	X
5. Estimation	X		X	X		X		X		X	X		X
6. Number Sense and Numeration	X	X	X	X	X			X	X	X	X	X	X
7. Concepts of Whole Number Operations		X	X	X	X			X	X	X	X		X
8. Whole Number Computation		X	X	X	X			X	X	X	X	X	X
9. Geometry and Spatial Sense			X	X		X	X			X		X	
10. Measurement	X		X	X						X	X	X	
11. Statistics and Probability	X	X						X	X		X	X	X
12. Fractions and Decimals					X			X	X	X			X
13. Patterns and Relationships	X	X	X	X	X	X	X	X	X	X	X	X	X
*14. Discrete Mathematics		X									X	X	X
*15. Algebra			X										
*16. Proof	X			X					X		X	X	X

*Note: these are not K-4 NCTM *Standards*.

certain ideas from algebra and discrete mathematics are indeed appropriate in the lower grades.

The third, proof, appears in several of the tasks. Even in fourth grade, children should be given opportunities to formulate simple but convincing arguments. Statements that begin like these:

"Johann could not *possibly* have gotten a 6 because . . . ."

"There are *exactly* eight different three-block towers that can be made from two colors because . . . ."

"You *can't* make a hexaright with an area of 36 cm^2 and a perimeter of 24 cm because . . . ."

can be completed in ways that amount to informal proofs.

The Future

These prototypes reveal just one aspect of the unfolding picture of reform in mathematics assessment. Both the NCTM and the MSEB are currently engaged in further efforts to promote standards-based assessment. NCTM is preparing assessment standards to complement earlier standards for curriculum and instruction. MSEB, in a parallel effort, is examining measurement and policy issues involved in various forms of assessment. In addition, advances in mathematics assessment are being made in many states across the nation.

Where do we go from here?

The messages conveyed by the prototypes in *Measuring Up* are consonant with the national goal of standards-based educational reform. In no way, however, do these prototypes provide definitive answers to the very deep and difficult issues surrounding assessment in mathematics education. The goal of *Measuring Up* is more modest: to further reform by providing rich examples that can be discussed and debated, refined, and improved. Through these prototypes we can glimpse the future of assessment in America.

Prototypes

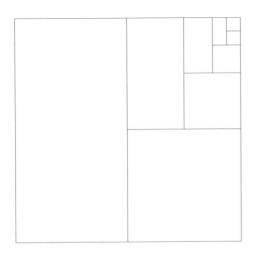

Mystery Graphs

Suggested time allotment
Less than one class period

Student social organization
Students working alone

Task

Assumed background: This task assumes that the children have had extensive experience in dealing with sets of data, and, in particular, are familiar with interpreting data that are represented in line plots.

Presenting the task: The teacher should distribute the student materials and read enough of it to be sure that the children understand the task. It is also important to stress that the "classroom of fourth graders" is some other classroom — not theirs. In the pilot, it was necessary to clarify that "cavities" in question 1a refers to both filled and unfilled cavities.

Student assessment activity: See the following pages.

Name _____ **Date** _____

Look at the five graphs on the next pages. Each graph shows something about a classroom of fourth graders.

1. Which of the five graphs do you think shows:

    a. The number of cavities that the fourth graders have? _____

    b. The ages of the fourth graders' mothers? _____

    c. The heights of the fourth graders, in inches? _____

    d. The number of people in the fourth graders' families? _____

2. Explain why you think the graph you picked for **c** is the one that shows the heights of fourth graders.

3. Why do you think the other graphs <u>don't</u> show the fourth graders' heights?

Graph 1

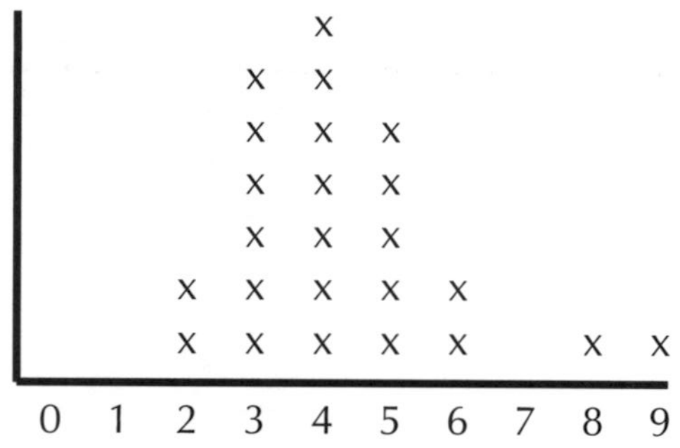

```
                    x
              x     x
        x     x     x
        x     x     x
        x     x     x
        x     x     x     x     x
  x     x     x     x     x     x
  x     x     x     x     x     x           x     x
  0     1     2     3     4     5     6     7     8     9
```

Graph 2

```
                                    x
                              x     x
                        x     x     x     x
                  x     x     x     x     x     x
                  x     x     x     x     x     x           x
  x               x     x     x     x     x     x     x     x     x
 55 56 57 58 59 60 61 62 63 64 65 66 67 68 69 70 71 72
```

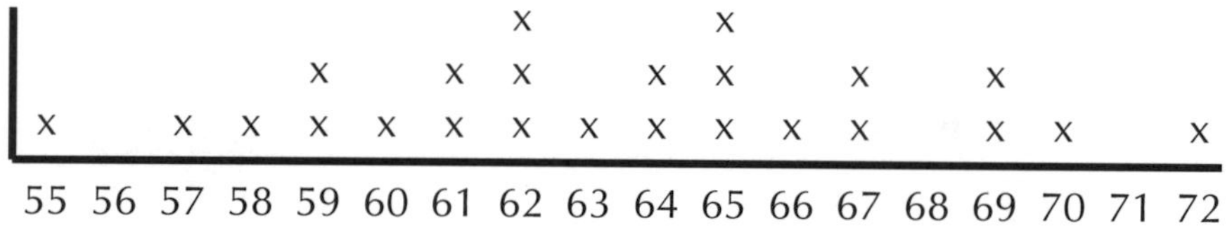

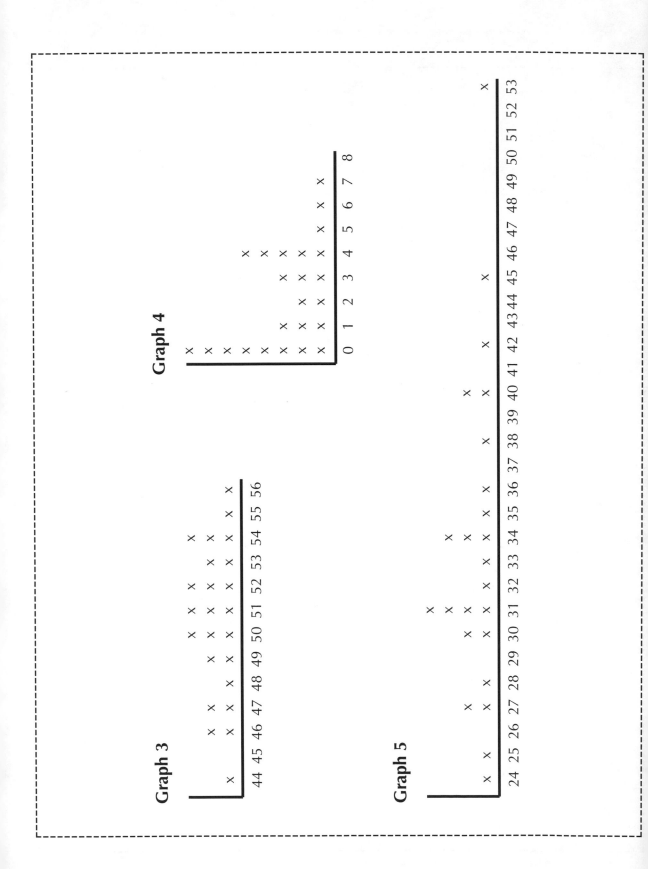

Rationale for the mathematics education community

This task puts a premium on looking at data sets, as opposed to individual pieces of information. This is a fundamental notion that should take an increasing role in the elementary mathematics curriculum. The task also gives children the opportunity to relate the graphical representations to their own experiences as fourth graders.

Ordinarily, of course, one would want children to have plenty of chances to collect, display, and analyze their own data, as the NCTM *Standards* suggest. If the task is going to fit within a single class period, however, there is not enough time to create five graphs for comparison. As a result, this task uses data that have already been collected from some hypothetical fourth grade. Clearly other assessment tasks (like the Hog Game and Buttons tasks in this collection) must include the collection, display, and analysis of data.

Task design considerations: Children seem naturally interested in data about people, particularly people of their own ages; this is one reason for choosing a hypothetical fourth-grade class as the basis of these data. The children will naturally bring their *own* experiences with heights, ages, family size, and dental health with them to the task. When using such situations for assessment purposes, one must be careful to use values of the data to which all the students can relate equally well. There may be cultural variations in family sizes or in the ages of fourth-graders' mothers, for example. To take this into account, the ranges of Graphs 1 and 5 are large enough to encompass every student's own family size and mother's age.

Questions similar to the one about heights could be asked about mothers' ages, family sizes, or cavities. The only reason such questions are not included is to save assessment time; the intent was to give an example of a task that could be done in less than one class period.

To some extent, this is a task that measures children's prior knowledge about the real world — about how many inches tall they are, how old their mothers are, and so on. If one is concerned with children's abilities to connect mathematics with their world of experience, this is a reasonable expectation.

The style of drawing line plots should be the same as the style to which the student is accustomed.

Ideally, the five graphs should be displayed so that the student can see them all at once.

Variants and extensions: A natural instructional follow-up to this task is to ask the students to compile data on heights, cavities, etc., from their own class, to compare with the data given.

Using just the data presented here, one could pose problems like: "Suppose Graph 2 really did show heights in inches. Whose heights could they be?" "Suppose Graph 3 showed the ages of the mothers of students in some grade level in our school. Which grade could that be?" "What other kinds of data could Graph 1 be showing?"

Protorubric

Characteristics of the high response:

High

I chose 3 for the heights because were about 4 or 5 feet tall and thats the number of inches from 44 to 56 would make sense

Question 2

The other ones dont show hights in 1 its too short only 2 inches tall! And 2 is someone is 72 inches thats 6 feet tall. 4 wouldn't be right because nobody can be 0 anything tall and 5 is too short too — like someone is 2 feet

Question 3

The high response shows a full understanding of the relationship between the graphs and the data they represent.

The responses for question 1 are all correct (a. 4; b. 5; c. 3; d. 1). Questions 2 and 3, taken together, should explain that Graph 3 shows a reasonable range of fourth graders' heights, and that ranges of data in the other graphs are not as reasonable. The only real alternative candidate for the heights is Graph 2, but that would imply that there are fourth graders who are six feet tall.

Characteristics of the medium response:

Graph 1 and Graph 4 are interchanged (number of cavities and number of family members); or Graph 2 is used in place of Graph 3 or Graph 5; or Graphs 3 and 5 are interchanged. Nonetheless, graphs showing the correct general orders of magnitude are selected. Some portions of the student's justifications are reasonable.

> Medium
>
> *Graph 2 is for the heights — a fourth grader could be 55 inches tall*
>
> Question 2
>
> *Graphs 1 and 4 are much to short*
>
> Question 3

Characteristics of the low response:

At most one graph is chosen that shows totally unrealistic data (e.g., Graph 5, with a range from 24 to 53, is selected for the number of people in the families). Responses to questions 2 and 3 are missing or indicate that the student cannot interpret the graphs, or they do not show any reasonable sense of the magnitudes of more than one of the items.

> Low
>
> *#1 could be hights — there are lots of Xs and that's the hights —*
>
> Question 2
>
> *The others can't be hights because #1 is the hights*
>
> Question 3

Reference

An earlier version of this task was developed by TERC (Cambridge, MA) for Education Development Center (Newton, MA).

The Checkers Tournament

Suggested time allotment
One class period

Student social organization
Students working alone or in pairs

Task

Assumed background: This task presents information in the form of a direct-

> *Broaden the view of mathematics appropriate for the 4th grade*
>
> *Translate information from one form to another*
>
> *Count without usual representations*
>
> *Deduce information presented as a graph*

ed graph, which is a way of showing relationships among objects. In this case, the dots represent people; they are connected with arrows indicating a certain mathematical relation: an arrow from A to B means "A won the game that A and B played." Some groups of children, for example ones that use the Comprehensive School Mathematics Program (McREL, 1992), will be familiar with a similar notation, and hence will need little teacher introduction. The task, however, does not assume familiarity with the notation. (Clearly it would be inappropriate to use this task to compare classes to whom this notation is familiar with classes to whom it is not.)

Children should have had some prior experience in "translating" from one

symbolic representation of a situation to another. In this case, the directed graph representation is to be transformed into a list of players ordered on the basis of their tournament records so far.

Presenting the task: If students are not already familiar with the directed graph notation, the teacher should introduce it (without the terminology "directed graph") as a means of displaying information about four students in a Tic-Tac-Toe tournament.

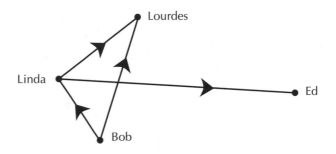

The teacher should explain the situation and ask simple questions such as:

Which students has Linda played? [Lourdes, Ed and Bob.]
Which games did she win? [The ones against Lourdes and Ed.]
Which games did she lose? [The one against Bob.]
Find two students who have not played against each other yet. [Lourdes and Ed; Ed and Bob.]
Who has played the fewest games? [Ed, with only one game played so far.]

Student assessment activity: The teacher should pass out copies of the student sheet and read through the introduction and question 1, to be sure that everyone has an understanding of the meaning of the dots and the arrows. A Spanish translation of the task appears immediately following the English version.

Name _____   **Date** _____

Six children are in a checkers tournament. The figure below shows the results of the games played so far.

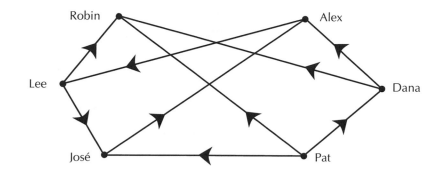

(Remember, in the picture, an arrow like

means that José won his game against Alex. The arrow always points <u>from</u> the winner <u>to</u> the loser.)

1. Who won the game between Pat and Robin? _____

2. Which children has Lee already played against? _____

3. Which of those games did Lee win? _____

4. How many games have been played by the children so far? _____
Explain how you know.

5. Make a table showing the current standings of the six children. Put the player who has won the most games in first place, at the top. If two players are tied, they can be listed in either order.

	Name	Wins	Losses
1.	_____	_____	_____
2.	_____	_____	_____
3.	_____	_____	_____
4.	_____	_____	_____
5.	_____	_____	_____
6.	_____	_____	_____

6. The tournament will be over when everybody has played everybody else exactly once. How many more games need to be played to finish the tournament? _____ Explain your answer.

7. Dana and Lee have not played yet. Who do you think will win when they play? _____ Explain why you think so.

Seis niños participan en un torneo de Damas. El dibujo representa los resultados de los partidos que han sido jugados hasta el momento.

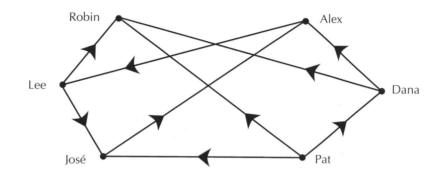

(Recuerda que en el dibujo una flecha como esta

significa que José le ganó el partido a Alex. La flecha siempre senala del ganador al perdedor.)

1. ¿Quién ganó el partido entre Pat y Robin? _____

2. ¿Contra qué niños ya ha jugado Lee? _____

3. ¿Cuál o cuáles de esos partidos ganó Lee? _____

4. ¿Cuántos partidos en total han jugado todos los niños hasta el momento? _____ Explica tu contestación.

5. Haz una tabla que demuestre la posición de los seis niños. Coloca al jugador o jugadora que ha ganado la mayor cantidad de partidos en el primer lugar; en la primera línea. Si hay un empate entre dos jugadores, puedes colocarlos en cualquier orden.

	Nombre	Partidos ganados	Partidos perdidos
1.	_____	_____	_____
2.	_____	_____	_____
3.	_____	_____	_____
4.	_____	_____	_____
5.	_____	_____	_____
6.	_____	_____	_____

6. El torneo terminará cuando todo el mundo haya jugado contra todo el mundo exactamente una vez. ¿Cuántos partidos faltan por jugar para que el torneo termine? Explica tu contestación.

7. Dana y Lee no han jugado todavía. ¿Quién crees que ganará cuando jueguen? _____ Explica el por qué tu piensas así.

Rationale for the mathematics education community

The content involved in this task is the elementary use of a network in graph theory to present a familiar situation. Such mathematics broadens the curriculum usually thought appropriate for the fourth grade. Yet the task is linked to more traditional material as students are asked to convert the graphical representation to a familiar ranked table, thus illustrating the connections between such different representations. The last two questions, in particular, allow a variety of strategies to be applied. Students must use analytical skills and demonstrate reasoning to answer the questions, two fundamental attributes of mathematical power. In addition, the task shows that mathematics can be non-computational.

One interesting feature of this task is that it requires children to count sets of objects (the games that have been played and the games that have yet to be played) when it is not immediately clear how these objects are represented in the given picture. Students are thus asked to explore a very basic notion — counting, in this instance — in a new context. When counting the games that have been played, the student may realize that each of the six players has played three games, because there are three arrows associated with each dot; nonetheless, it is not true that 18 games have been played. (The student must see the one-to-one correspondence between the arrows and the games, and devise a way to count the arrows properly, keeping track of which arrows have been counted and which have not, or simply realize that each game has a winner and loser, and divide 18 by 2.) It is even more challenging to count the games that have *not* yet been played.

Task design considerations: Note that the relation "X beats Y in a game of checkers" is not transitive; that is, if X beats Y and Y beats Z, then it is not necessarily the case that X beats Z. In fact, the games were deliberately arranged so that one trio of players illustrates this: José beat Alex and Alex beat Lee, but José did not beat Lee.

An earlier version of question 6 was phrased as "How many games need to be played to finish the tournament?" This was found to be somewhat ambiguous; it could mean either "How many games in all are needed?" or "How many more games are needed?" Children in a pilot test interpreted the question in both ways. Because there was nothing to be gained by the ambiguity, it is now "How many more games need to be played to finish the tournament?"

The Spanish translation of the task is included to highlight the need for assessment designers and teachers to be sensitive to the nuances of language. This translation, like the one of the Taxman task, has been done in the informal form. Some students (for example, those from Costa Rica) will not be used to this form. Also, note that question 3, "Which of those games did Lee win?" has been translated as "¿Cuál o cuáles de esos partidos ganó Lee?" Using only "cuál" or "cuáles" by itself would prejudge the situation by telling the student whether there is one game or more than one.

Variants and extensions: Several variants come to mind immediately. One can add players, add or change the directions of the arrows, and ask other kinds of questions — for example, "If there were 7 players, how many games would there be if everyone played everyone else exactly once?"

One can extend the setting to relations that are transitive — for example, an arrow pointing from A to B means that "A is taller than B." This relation, unlike the one in this task, is transitive, and so one can infer that if there are arrows from A to B and from B to C, then there must be an arrow from A to C.

Indeed, there are dozens of variations on the theme of presenting information about relations among objects through the use of arrow diagrams (directed graphs). These objects can be numbers, geometric figures, or other mathematical entities, as well as people.

Protorubric

Characteristics of the high response:

The high-level response is one that shows an understanding of the situation as a whole — what the various components of the directed graph represent, and how that representation relates to the other representation.

One expects that all answers will be correct. In question 4, the justification for asserting that 9 games have been played so

> High
>
> dana will win I think. Because dana has played (according to the result) better people even thogh, they have the # of games won and lost, like dana played pat and pat wins all the tim That was the only tim dana lost,
>
> Question 7
>
> I think Dana Will win because She beat Alex and Lee lost to Alex
>
> Question 7
>
> ?? Predict who's going to win You can't → because the both have the Same record — or maybe it will be a tie
>
> Question 7

far is something to the effect that (a) there are 9 arrows or that (b) each of 6 players has competed in 3 games, which means a total of 18 wins and losses. Since each game produces a win and a loss, there must have been 9 games.

Note that in question 5, ties arise for 2nd and 3rd places in the ranking, as well as for 4th and 5th. Therefore, either order within those pairs is correct.

In question 6, the correct answer, 6, can be obtained by enumerating the pairs who have not played. Alternately, the child may see that there will be a total of 15 games, and, since 9 have been played, 6 remain.

In question 7, the rationale could be any of the following:

a. Since Dana beat Alex and Alex beat Lee, I think Dana will beat Lee.

b. Since both Dana and Lee have identical 2-1 records, we cannot predict who will win.

c. Dana and Lee have identical 2-1 records, but Dana lost to Pat, the best player at 3-0, while Lee lost to Jose, whose record is only 1 win, 2 losses. Therefore, Dana seems to be the stronger player, and so I think Dana will win.

If one were to make finer distinctions within the "high" category, it is important to note that response a, above, makes an argument that is not fully justified by the situation. As already mentioned, the relation is *not* transitive, and hence the outcome of the Dana-Lee game is not necessarily a win by Dana. So "I think Dana will beat Lee" is a better response than simply "Dana will beat Lee."

Characteristics of the medium response:

The student can interpret the meaning of individual arrows correctly and can determine how many games have been played so far. Thus questions 1 through 4 are mostly answered correctly. The response to question 5, however, indicates difficulty in connecting the arrow-diagram notation with the table showing the standings of the players. One or two pairs of names may be in the incorrect order.

Medium

> 10 games. Because there are
> 6 Players in the tournament each
> of them have to play each other once
> So each of them have to
> play 2 games 5x2=10
> There is only 5 games because
> they don't play there self.

Question 6

> 12 games. There are six kids therefor
> everybody has to play five times and they have only played
> three times they each have to play two more times to
> have played everybody. 5-3=2 and 2x6=12. So 12
> more games have to be played.

Question 6

In question 6, the child may erroneously conclude that a total of 30 games will be played (6 people, 5 games each) and hence give an answer of 21. This answer shows greater insight than one that is closer to the correct answer but was obtained by incorrectly counting the missing arrows.

The rationale offered in question 7 is based on a correct interpretation of some of the information presented in the arrow diagram, but does not present any kind of complete argument. For example, the student may say something like, "Dana, because Dana beat Alex," or "Lee, because Lee beat two people," or "You can't tell, because they both lost to Robin."

Characteristics of the low response:

Questions 1 through 3 are answered correctly. However, there is little awareness of the relationship between the arrows in the diagram and the games that have been played. Hence responses to questions 4 through 6 are incorrect or lack any kind of justification.

The response to question 7 may be based on subjective feelings that have no basis in the information supplied in the arrow diagram. For example, the child may say something like "Dana, because I think she's better."

Reference

Mid-continent Regional Educational Laboratory (1992). *Comprehensive School Mathematics Program.* Aurora (CO): Author.

Bridges

Suggested time allotment
Two class periods

Student social organization
Students working alone

Task

Assumed background: It is assumed that the students have had prior experience with using standard colored centimeter rods (or the equivalent). The task also assumes that the children have had experience with "rules" (functions) that describe a general numerical situation.

Presenting the task: Students are given an assortment of colored rods and a copy of the student pages. As always, calculators should be available. The teacher should present the task essentially as the "script" below specifies.

43

"You are an engineer who wants to build different kinds of bridges. The bridges will be made of colored rods. The first bridge you are to build is a 1-span bridge made with one yellow rod and two red rods." (Build the bridge illustrated below, with the students copying.) "The yellow rod is called a *span,* and the red rods are called *supports.* Since the yellow rod is 5 cm long, the length of the bridge is 5 cm."

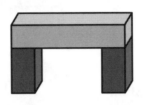

"The second bridge you are to build is a 2-span bridge made with two yellow rods and four red rods (as shown below). Note that this bridge is 10 cm long."

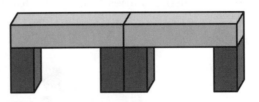

"As you build bridges in the following activities, think of a way to keep track of the number of rods of different colors you use. Your goal is to find out how many rods of each color you would need to build a bridge of *any* size."

Student assessment activity: Distribute the activity sheet and read through question 1 to be sure that the children understand the basic problem. Note: the bridges have been scaled to fit the 7" x 10" page of this volume. The teacher may choose to redraw the bridges to scale when they are reproduced on standard size paper

Part 1

All of the bridges in Part 1 are built with yellow rods for spans and red rods for supports, like the one shown here. This is a 2-span bridge like the one you just built. Note that the yellow rods are 5 cm long.

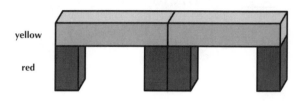

1. Now, build a 3-span bridge.

   a. How many yellow rods did you use? _____

   b. How long is your bridge? _____

   c. How many red rods did you use? _____

   d. How many rods did you use altogether? _____

2. Try to answer these questions without building a 5-span bridge. If you want, build a 5-span bridge to check your answers.

   a. How many yellow rods would you need for a 5-span bridge? _____

   b. How long would your bridge be? _____

   c. How many red rods would you need? _____

   d. How many rods would you need altogether? _____

3. Without building a 12-span bridge, answer the following questions.

   a. How many yellow rods would you need for a 12-span bridge? _____

   b. How long would your bridge be? _____

   c. How many red rods would you need? _____

   d. How many rods would you need altogether? _____

4. How many yellow rods and red rods would you need to build a 28-span bridge? _____ yellow rods and _____ red rods. Explain your answer.

5. Write a rule for figuring out the total number of rods you would need to build a bridge if you knew how many spans the bridge had.

6. How many yellow rods and red rods would you need to build a bridge that is 185 cm long? _____ yellow rods and _____ red rods. Explain your answer.

Name _____ **Date** _____

Part 2

The bridges for this part are built like this 2-span bridge:

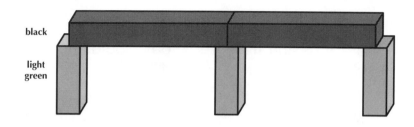

The black rods are 7 cm long, and the light green rods are 3 cm long. Notice that the supports are <u>shared</u> between spans, except at the ends.

1. Build a 3-span bridge of this same kind, with black and light green.

   a. How many black rods did you use? _____

   b. How long is your bridge? _____

   c. How many light green rods did you use? _____

   d. How many rods did you use altogether? _____

2. Try to answer these questions without building a 5-span bridge. If you want to, build a 5-span bridge to check your answers.

   a. How many black rods would you need for a 5-span bridge?_____

   b. How long would your bridge be? _____

   c. How many light green rods would you need? _____

   d. How many rods would you need altogether? _____

3. Without building a 13-span bridge, answer the following questions.

    a. How many black rods would you need for a 13-span bridge?_____

    b. How long would your bridge be? _____

    c. How many light green rods would you need? _____

    d. How many rods would you need altogether? _____

4. How many black rods and light green rods would you need to build a 56-span bridge? _____ black rods and _____ light green rods. Explain your answer.

5. Write a rule for figuring out how many rods you would need to build a bridge if you knew how many spans the bridge had.

6. How many black rods and light green rods would you need to build a bridge that is at least 429 cm long? _____ black rods and _____ light green rods. Explain your answer.

Rationale for the mathematics education community

The Bridges task illustrates how manipulative materials can be used as an integral part of an assessment task. Such tasks may encourage and support the use of concrete materials in day-to-day instruction, as called for in the NCTM *Standards.*

The task also focuses on the generation and identification of patterns in a numerical setting, and especially on organizing information — "keeping track" — to find patterns. The child might create a table showing, for example, that 1 span requires 3 rods; 2 spans require 5 rods; and so forth. Then the child might generalize to 13, or 56, or N spans. Thus there is a progression from building a simple structure, to predicting what a more complex structure would look like, and then to generalizing to an arbitrary case.

Furthermore, it is significant that arithmetic computation — rather than being an end in and of itself — is used in the service of answering questions about the bridges. The task is designed so that a variety of approaches to the computation are feasible — calculator, mental, or traditional paper-and-pencil algorithms. More important than the computation itself, however, are the students' decisions about what computations are appropriate, and the connection between the computation and the dimensions of the bridges.

Task design considerations: The directions are phrased so as to encourage the child to use the physical materials as needed to understand the situation, and then to move beyond them. As always, the aim is to encourage self-monitoring: children should be able to decide for themselves what they need to do to understand the situation. Thus sentences are worded like, "If you want, build a 5-span bridge to check your answers."

Note that the picture in Part 2 shows the light green rod on each end of the bridge displaced so that one half centimeter juts out beyond the black rods. This is done to be sure the student realizes that even in a longer bridge each light green rod except the ones on the end supports two black rods. (If the light green rods were moved in a half centimeter, so that they were flush with the ends of the black rods, the student might think that the entire configuration shown in the picture is to be repeated.) As a result, one should be alert for the child who interprets the length of the bridge to be one centimeter more than the sum of the lengths of the black rods; for example, the bridge shown could be thought of as being 15 cm long. Such an interpretation would be completely reasonable.

The size of the numbers in question 6 of Part 1 and Part 2 were chosen carefully. Although 185 (in Part 1) may seem too large, it may be easier than a smaller number. The reason is that fourth graders may tend to rely on familiar addition and subtraction techniques. The students will approach question 6 of Part 1 by writing a long column of "5"s, appending more and more "5"s until the sum reaches 185. The smaller the target number, the more likely it is that this technique will be used, (and the more likely it is to be successful). While there is nothing mathematically "wrong" with this approach, educators want students to move beyond it. So one motivation for using a number as large as 185 is to encourage the child to think of an easier, more efficient, way to tackle the problem. By using the larger number, the assessor can get a richer picture of what the student can do. Similar comments can be made about the numbers in question 4 of both Parts.

Question 6 of Part 2 is different from the others in its use of "at least" and in the fact that 429 is not a multiple of 7. The number was chosen because the division is fairly easy to do mentally (420 divided by 7 is 60, and then two more black rods are needed to get beyond 429, for a total of 62 black rods). Of course students who do not see a way to perform the calculations mentally are free to use a calculator — although they will have to deal with the resulting decimal!

The amount of time that this kind of task requires is very much dependent on the students' prior experiences. Children who are very familiar with using centimeter rods to model situations like building bridges, or who have extensive experience in abstracting general "rules" may need significantly less time to do this task than children whose mathematical backgrounds are not as rich. For some classes, then, one full period may be sufficient time.

Variants and extensions: One straightforward set of variants can be obtained by varying the numbers in the task, or the rod sizes used, or the way in which an individual span is constructed. For example, each span might have three upright support rods, and each horizontal piece might consist of two rods of the same color, one on top of the other. This is a setting in which children can invent their own styles of bridges and their own questions about them.

More generally, bridge-building with centimeter rods can be used to explore other mathematical topics — for example, in the area of primes and factors: "Can you build a bridge that is exactly 101 cm long, using spans of the same length?" or "Can you build two parallel bridges of the same length, one using 6-cm rods and the other using 8-cm rods; if so, how long might the bridges be?"

Protorubric

Characteristics of the high response:

The high response shows that the child can make a transition between the physical materials and the more abstract arithmetical ideas.

All questions are answered correctly. The rules described in question 5 of Parts 1 and 2 clearly describe a general case, that is, how one would find the total number of rods for any number of spans. This can be done through words or through symbols, or a combination of both. Some children may not explicitly mention the spans; for example, they might simply write "multiply by 3" for question 5 of Part 1.

High

Each yellow rod has 2 red rods so all you do is double the number of yellow rods to figure out how many red rods their are. So Add the number of spans and that same number doubled for the answer.

Question 5 (Part 1)

62 BL   7 goes into 429 61
63 LG   times and something more. So you have to have 62 is the number of the black rods. There is always one more LG red than black rod –

Question 6 (Part 2)

The justifications in question 6 in both parts are detailed. For example, in Part 1, the explanation indicates that 185 was divided by 5, and that there are twice as many red rods as yellow rods. If a calculator is used in question 6 of Part 2, the decimal result is interpreted correctly.

Characteristics of the medium response:

Medium

if the bridge was 5 spans long
you would need 5 yellow and 10 reds

Question 5 (Part 1)

Questions 1 through 4 of Parts 1 and 2 are answered satisfactorily — that is, a pattern has been noted and extended to the bridges that are too long to construct with the available rods.

Questions 5 and 6, however, are not answered appropriately; the general rule may be unclear or not universally applicable.

In Part 2, if the division of 429/7 is done using a calculator (or with pencil and paper), the resulting decimal is reported without rounding up to the next whole number.

Characteristics of the low response:

Low

You would need 16 yellow rods & 18 red rods
to make a span bridge.

Question 5 (Part 1)

You need 189 rods. First you count the
yellow rod by 5 and then you draw a
picher with 185 cm. so you will know how
many Rods you need.

Question 6 (Part 1)

Questions 1 and 2 of Parts 1 and 2 are answered satisfactorily, although the child may have to build the 5-span bridges and count the rods before responding.

More generally, though, the low response indicates an incomplete grasp of the relationships among (a) the length of each span rod, (b) the number of spans, and (c) the total length of the bridge.

Hexarights

Suggested time allotment
One class period

Student social organization
Students working alone or in pairs

Task

Assumed background:
This task assumes that the children are familiar with area and perimeter of plane figures and with perpendicular lines. In particular, the children should have had some experience in

- measuring lengths of line segments and in drawing right angles (using an L-square or similar tool)

- drawing objects (like rectangles) that meet predetermined criteria — for example with given areas or perimeters.

It is also assumed that the students have had some experience in dealing with newly defined geometric objects. The assessment activity does <u>not</u>, however, assume any familiarity with hexarights. Indeed, part of what is being assessed is children's abilities to grapple with a concept that is new to them.

Presenting the task: The teacher should first be sure that everyone recalls that a hexagon is a 6-sided plane figure, and that adjacent sides are sides that touch. Then he or she should distribute copies of the student sheet and read through the first item to ensure that everyone has a beginning understanding of what a hexaright is. As always, tools for drawing should be available for children to use as they see the need. The tools should include rulers, L-squares (which provide an easy way to draw right angles), centimeter tiles, and centimeter graph paper. An L-square is provided on the back cover of this book.

Student assessment activity: See the following pages. Note: the student work pages have been drawn to fit the 7" x 10" page of this volume. Reproduction of these pages for student use may affect the scale of the centimeter graph paper in questions 2 and 3 and the hexaright in question 4. The teacher may choose to redraw these diagrams to achieve proper scale.

We made up a new kind of shape and made up a name for it: hexaright. Here's the <u>definition</u>: A hexaright is a hexagon in which each pair of adjacent sides is perpendicular.

Here are some examples of hexarights:

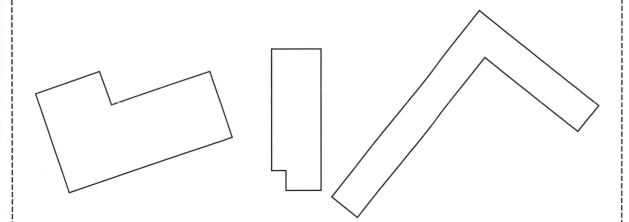

This is not a hexaright because not all pairs of adjacent sides are perpendicular.

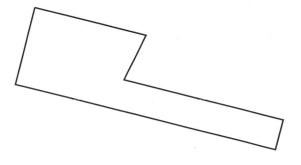

1. This is not a hexaright either.   Why not?

2. This hexaright has been drawn on some centimeter graph paper. Find the <u>perimeter</u> and the <u>area</u> of this hexaright:

Perimeter:_____   Area: _____

3. This hexaright has also been drawn on some centimeter graph paper. Find the <u>perimeter</u> and <u>area</u> of this hexaright:

Perimeter:_____   Area: _____

4. Here's a hexaright with a perimeter of 24 cm.

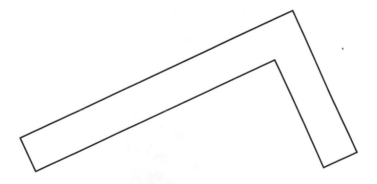

What is the <u>area</u> of this hexaright? _____

5. There are lots of different hexarights with a perimeter of 24 cm. On a separate piece of paper, draw two <u>different</u> hexarights, each one with a perimeter of 24 cm. (Be sure to put your name on the paper!)

6. Draw one more hexaright with perimeter 24 cm, and <u>make the area as large as you can</u>. You can draw it in the space below or on another piece of paper.

What is the area of the hexaright you just drew? _____

7. What did you find out about the areas of hexarights with a perimeter of 24 cm?

Rationale for the mathematics education community

An important feature of this task is that it incorporates basic ideas from geometry and measurement — perpendicularity, line segments, area, perimeter — to define a new geometric figure previously unknown to students — hexarights. It is not, however, hexarights in and of themselves that are important. Rather, it is the ability of students to use some familiar mathematical ideas to define and explore a new class of mathematical objects.

The purpose of the task is to assess how well students can deal with this new concept, in the sense of (a) being able to distinguish what fits the definition and what does not and (b) constructing examples that fulfill given constraints.

The ideas suggested by hexarights are particularly rich from a mathematical standpoint. The task provides an opportunity for students to explore the idea of maximizing one property — area in this case — while keeping other properties — perimeter here — fixed. Again, it is neither hexarights nor area and perimeter that make the task noteworthy; it is the mathematical investigation of interrelated properties that is an important part of mathematical power. Similarly, the task asks students to think about what hexarights are not. The point is that the little "bite" that makes the figure a hexaright (rather than a rectangle) can be made as small as one wishes; but once the bite disappears, so too does the hexaright! Hence, while the area can be arbitrarily close to 36 cm^2, it cannot equal 36 cm^2.

Still another important reason for including this task is that the students are given the opportunity to select the tools that they need or want to use to do the drawings. Some children will prefer to use paper ruled in centimeters (which in fact may limit their drawings to hexarights with integral sides); others will use a centimeter L-square, which is a very appropriate tool in this case. It is important for teachers and texts to leave the selection of tools for particular tasks to the students, particularly by the time they reach fourth grade. The selection of the proper tool from several possibilities is a vital part of problem-solving because each tool may have its own advantages and disadvantages in a given setting.

Task design considerations: Several features of this task deserve highlighting:

Note that hexarights are formally defined in words, as opposed to being implicitly "defined" *solely* through lots of examples and non-examples. (Of course it may well be that some children of this age will form the "hexaright" concept through the pictures rather than through the words. If the task were used with older children, it might be appropriate to convey the concept without the pictures. The students would then be expected to generate whatever pictures they would need to solidify the concept in their own minds.) Note also that the shape was intentionally given a name that suggests its meaning, rather than an invented nonsense word (as is typical of some materials that aim at concept formation through examples and non-examples).

All the pictures of hexarights are drawn so their sides are not parallel with the edges of the paper. This is in an effort to combat one of the most prevalent misconceptions about geometry: that the properties of being a rectangle or square, or (more generally) the relations of parallel and perpendicular have something to do with the orientation of the lines with respect to the edges of the page or the chalkboard. Even in the cases of questions 2 and 3, the pieces of centimeter graph paper are shown as if they had been torn from a larger sheet and placed obliquely with respect to the edges of the page.

Question 5 deliberately does not leave sufficient space to answer the question, and instead calls for the student to use a separate piece of paper. The purpose of this is to force the child to decide what kind of paper to use. Centimeter graph paper will be helpful to some students and a distraction for others.

Similarly, in question 7, no lines are provided for the student to write on. Some children will want to describe their findings in words, while others will want to explain via pictures. No method is best a priori. (Students should be encouraged to use a sheet of lined paper, however, if they ask to do so.) Filling the page with lines to write on might convey the message that pictures are not appropriate.

A note on the definition of "hexaright": Although three technical words are involved in the definition — "hexagon," "adjacent," and "perpendicular" — they are all useful in a variety of settings, mathematical and non-mathematical. In any case, teachers are asked to make sure everyone understands these terms.

Notice also the introductory sentence that says that "hexaright" is a made-up term. One would also not want teachers or other adults to think that a hexaright is some concept from high school geometry that they have forgotten!

An alternative would have been to define the hexaright as a hexagon all of whose angles are right angles. Some may object to this form of the definition, thinking that "angle" connotes "interior angle." Since the measure of one interior angle of a hexaright is 270°, confusion might result.

Variants and extensions: The difficulty of the task can be varied by asking intermediate questions. For example, even before question 1, the student might be asked to draw some hexarights (without size conditions) or to describe in their own words what hexarights look like.

One variant of the task is to use numbers that are not integers for the areas or perimeters of the figures. This might help some children to see that there is no largest hexaright with a perimeter of 24 cm; for others, however, the task would become more difficult.

A natural extension of the task is to consider octarights (or, more generally, polyrights) and their areas and perimeters. Interestingly, octarights occur in three basic shapes (as opposed to hexarights' single basic L-shape).

An extension in another direction is to consider the 3-dimensional analog of a hexaright. If a rectangular box in 3 dimensions is the analog of a rectangle in 2 dimensions, what does the 3-dimensional analog of a hexaright look like? What are the corresponding roles of volume and surface area?

Protorubric

Characteristics of the high response:

The high-level response is one that demonstrates an overall facility for dealing with the newly-defined hexaright, and that shows some understanding of the complementary roles of perimeter and area in the task — that is, that there are hexarights with perimeter 24 cm and areas that are very close (but not equal) to 36 square centimeters.

The student's responses to questions 1 through 4 are correct, although the indications of "cm" and "square cm" (or "cm^2") may be missing.

The hexarights drawn for questions 5 and 6 are close to being completely accurate, with virtually right angles and side lengths within 0.5 cm of being correct. (An alternative, which in some ways is more sophisticated, is a sketch, drawn without a straightedge, that indicates clearly the dimensions.) The area of the hexaright for question 6 is accurate, is at least 34 square cm, and is as large as the ones in question 5.

The highest level response to question 7 says something to the effect that there is no hexaright with perimeter 24 cm and area 36 cm^2. (No fourth grader should be expected to justify this fact completely.) Full credit should be

High

24 CM

Question 5

This is 35 square cm big

It can be even bigger if you make this part smaller.

You could make it like this or littler than that even.

Question 6

given to any response that refers to a square of perimeter 24 cm, or that says there are hexarights of perimeter 24 cm and area arbitrarily close to 36 cm^2. Somewhat less is assigned to a response that simply refers to some (finite) sequence of hexarights of perimeter 24 cm and increasing area.

Characteristics of the medium response:

The responses to questions 1-4 show an understanding of what a hexaright is and what the perimeter and area are. There may be a flaw in one of the calculations. The responses to question 5 provides supporting evidence of understanding, if there are any miscalculations.

> Medium
>
> There are lots of ways to get hexrights with a perimeter of 24 cm. Some are diffrent sizes of areas.
>
> Question 7

The figures drawn in questions 5 and 6 are hexarights, although the lengths of the sides may be up to a centimeter wrong in either direction, the angles may not be accurately drawn right angles, and the perimeter may not be exactly 24 cm. (Of course the nature of the errors will depend on the kinds of tools, including type of paper, that the student selects.)

In question 6, the partial understanding that is typical of the medium-level response can be shown in a variety of ways. For example, the student could draw a hexaright with a relatively small area (perhaps 30 cm^2), but report the area accurately (within perhaps 1 cm^2 of the correct area). Alternatively, an appropriate hexaright could be drawn very well, but the area misidentified as 23 cm^2 rather than 35 cm^2.

The response to question 7 is something that is true (for example, that there are lots of hexarights of different areas, for a fixed perimeter) but that does not address any connections between or among hexarights with perimeter 24 cm.

Characteristics of the low response:

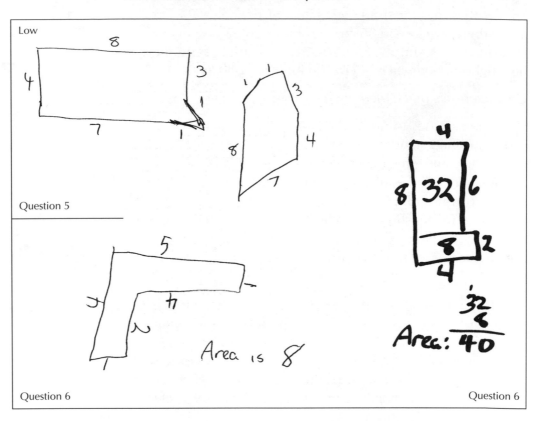

Low

Question 5

Question 6

Area is 8

Area: 40

Question 6

Little understanding evinced of what a hexaright is, and of what area and perimeter are. The drawings are done without regard to accuracy, either in making straight line segments or in making right angles. Moreover, the student's response to question 7 is not related to the problem in a low response.

Bowl-A-Fact

Suggested time allotment
One class period

Student social organization
Students working alone or in pairs, after short teacher introduction

Task

Assumed background: The problem assumes that the students have had some experience in using parentheses with arithmetic operations.

Presenting the task: The teacher explains that in bowling the objective is to knock down 10 pins with one or two throws of a bowling ball. Knocking down all 10 pins with one throw is called a strike. Knocking down all the pins in two throws is called a spare. The game of Bowl-A-Fact is similar to bowling, except instead of throwing a bowling ball, one tosses three number cubes (numbered from 1 through 6) and makes as many numbers from 1 to 10 as possible by adding, subtracting, multiplying or dividing the numbers showing on the number cubes. Each number showing on a number cube must be used exactly once on one side of an

equation. For each number that can be obtained, the corresponding circle is shaded. (This indicates a pin knocked down.)

Student assessment activity: After explaining the rules of Bowl-A-Fact, the teacher should play one game with the whole class. Pretend that the number cubes on the first toss were 3, 4, and 6. Individual students can devise number sentences to knock down pins that have been drawn on the board, as shown below.

Of course the pins will probably be knocked down in some order different from the one shown. Also, depending on a child's strategy, the pin number could be on the right or left side of the equals sign. For example, one child might ask, "What can I do with 3, 4 and 6?" and come up with "4 + 6 - 3 = 7," while another might ask, "Is there any way to knock down the 7 pin?" and write the equation "7 = 4 + 6 - 3."

Note, too, that there are other ways of getting many of the pin numbers; this should be explicitly pointed out.

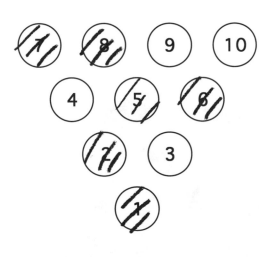

$$1 = 3 + 4 - 6$$
$$7 = 4 + 6 - 3$$
$$(3 \times 4) \div 6 = 2$$
$$6 = 6 \div (4 - 3)$$
$$8 = 4 \times (6 \div 3)$$
$$6 - (4 - 3) = 5$$

Now the teacher should ask the class to pretend that the next roll is 3, 3, and 4. This is sufficient to knock down the remaining pins, thus getting a spare.

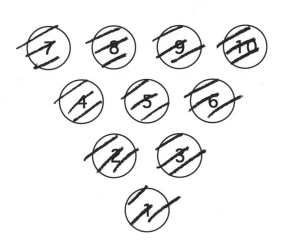

$$10 = 3 + 3 + 4$$
$$3 = 4 - (3 \div 3)$$
$$4 = 4 \times (3 \div 3)$$
$$9 = 3 \times 4 - 3$$

Students are given three number cubes and a copy of the following activity sheets.

Name _____ **Date** _____

1. Play a game of Bowl-A-Fact. Roll the three number cubes, and write the numbers you get in these spaces: _____ _____ _____ . (Roll again if you get 3, 4, 6 or 3, 3, 4) Use the numbers to knock down as many pins as you can. (For this part and the remaining parts, record your figuring in the spaces provided.)

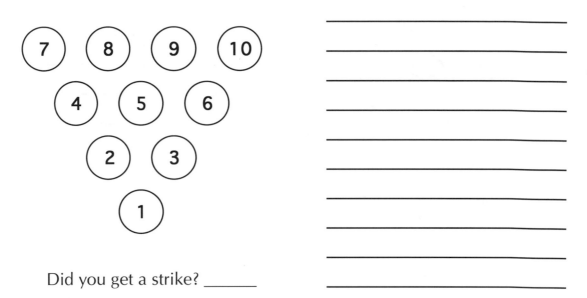

Did you get a strike? _____

_____

_____

_____

_____

_____

_____

_____

_____

_____

2. If you got a strike, go on to the next page. If you did <u>not</u> get a strike, try for a spare. Roll the three number cubes and write them here: _____ _____ _____ . Now use the new numbers to knock down as many of the remaining pins as you can.

_____   _____

_____   _____

_____   _____

_____   _____

_____   _____

3. Suppose you play again and the numbers you roll are 2, 3, and 6. Knock down as many pins as you can using these numbers.

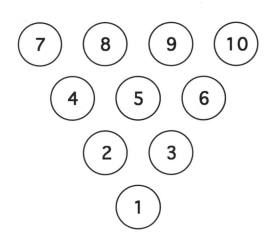

_____

_____

_____

_____

_____

_____

_____

_____

_____

Did you get a strike? _____

4. Suppose your next roll is 1, 3, and 5. Try to knock down the rest of the pins (get a spare) using these numbers.

_____   _____

_____   _____

_____   _____

_____   _____

_____   _____

Did you get a spare? _____

5. What pins can you knock down with this toss? 1, 2, and 4.

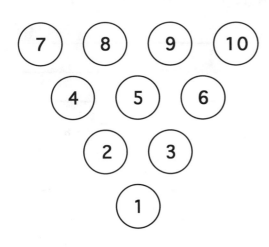

Did you get a strike? _____

Rationale for the mathematics education community

Bowl-A-Fact illustrates a purely arithmetic task in a setting that requires students to generate their own equations rather than merely compute answers to a given set of problems. It tests for facility with the number facts for all four operations using a form of exhaustive thinking. Students have to work backwards, asking themselves how they can combine the three given numbers to create the pin numbers.

What is the role of calculators in this activity? Calculators should be available to the students, as always, but it will soon become clear to them that calculators have very limited value in this situation. In fact, using a calculator to generate an equation to knock over pins is an extremely inefficient way to approach the task. Thus one reason for using these kinds of tasks is to sharpen students' perception of when calculators are useful and when they are not.

Another reason for including the task is that it so readily lends itself to subsequent instruction on combinatorics and probability, mathematical content not usually included in the fourth grade curriculum. (See the Variants and extensions section below.)

It is important to note that — with appropriate teacher guidance — the task illustrates that there can be more than one way to solve a problem; for instance, using 3, 4, and 6, one can knock over pin 2 by writing "$2 = (3 \times 4) \div 6$" or by writing "$2 = 4 - (6 \div 3)$." This will probably not be apparent to a student who is working alone, because he or she would have little need to consider alternative solutions for a pin value. That is, once a pin is knocked down, there is no point in doing it again. Instead, the idea should be conveyed in the teacher's introduction to the game, or in post-assessment follow-up discussions.

Task design considerations: This task is very much like the kind of game that would be useful as an instructional activity. Two features of the task are designed so that it is useful also as an assessment that could be used for comparative purposes.

One is that the teacher introduction will be exactly the same for all students and that introduction will illustrate all aspects of the game. The teacher specifies exactly what numbers are to be used in the demonstration for the whole class: 3, 4, and 6 for the first roll, followed by 3, 3, and 4. These numbers are carefully chosen to illustrate (a) what a spare and a strike are; (b) what to do if a number appears more than once among the three cubes; and (c) the use of division.

The second technique that is used because the task is intended for assessment is to allow children to play the game using whatever numbers they happen to roll in questions 1 and 2, followed by some predetermined rolls in the remaining questions. The results of questions 1 and 2 could be used by the teacher for diagnostic purposes, but they are not considered to be part of the formal assessment, and they are not discussed in the protorubric. (The reason, of course, is that the difficulty of the task depends on the numbers one happens to roll.)

Variants and extensions: There are many variants of the task, using different numbers on the cubes, different numbers on the pins, different numbers of cubes or of pins, different allowable operations (beyond addition, subtraction, multiplication, and division), and so forth. For example, one might want to try Super Bowl-A-Fact using 15 pins (from 1 through 15), four number cubes (each numbered from 1 through 6, as before), and change the rules so that the player can use the numbers from either three or four of the cubes. This is a good opportunity for students to make up their own variations on the game.

The game can be extended to a consideration of some questions in combinatorics and probability. For instance, "How many different ways are there to make a strike? What's the worst possible roll — or is there more than one? How many different rolls are possible with three number cubes? What's the probability of rolling a strike?" These questions lend themselves to longer projects; groups of students can organize the results of their investigations and present them to the rest of the class.

Protorubric

General notes: For the purposes of this protorubric, questions 1 and 2 are not included, for the reasons cited above.

In questions 3 and 4, here are the possibilities: With 2, 3, and 6, one can knock down the pins 4, 5, 6, 7, and 9. With 1, 3, and 5, one can knock down the pins 1, 2, 3, 7, 8, 9, and 10. Hence it is possible to make a spare, but not a strike, with the given rolls.

In question 5, however, one can knock down all the pins with 1, 2, and 4, so it is possible to get a strike.

Notice that one can obtain useful diagnostic information from children's incorrect equations. Consider, for example, these three incorrect equations (which might be given on question 1 or 2):

(a) $6 + 4 \div 2 = 5$

(b) $(6 \div 2) + 4 = 6$

(c) $(2 \div 6) + 4 = 7$

The child who writes (a) may not understand how and when parentheses are used; the child who writes (b) may have a problem with basic number facts; he may think either that $6 \div 2$ is 2 or that $3 + 4$ is 6. The child who writes (c) may fully understand that 6 divided by 2 is 3, but be confused about the order in which the operands are conventionally written. Errors such as these can be useful clues in understanding children's mathematical thinking.

Characteristics of the high response:

A high response shows flexibility of thinking. The use of parentheses is accurate, and the numbers obtained are correct. A spare is obtained in questions 3 and 4, and a strike in question 5.

The highest level of response would knock down all five possible pins in question 3, even though pins 7 and 9 could also be knocked down in the second roll.

Note that the questions do not ask for multiple ways of knocking down pins. The fact that

High

$1 + 2 + 4 = 7$
$1 - 2 + 4 = 3$
$1 \times 2 + 4 = 6$
$1 + 2 \times 4 = 9$
$1 \times 2 \times 4 = 8$
$1 = 4 - (1+2)$
$2 = 4 - (1 \times 2)$
$4 = 4 \times (2-1)$
$5 = 4 + (2-1)$
$10 = (4+1) \times 2$

Did you get a strike? __YES!__

Question 5

there is often more than one way to knock down a pin may be an interesting and attractive feature of this activity. But from the viewpoint of playing the game, once is enough!

Characteristics of the medium response:

The responses to questions 3, 4, and 5 include at most two incorrect equations, and at most two possible pins are omitted.

Characteristics of the low response:

The low response shows some understanding of basic arithmetic; at least five equations are written correctly. But there is apparently little flexibility of thought, because many of the pins that could be knocked over are left standing.

Reference

Shoecraft, Paul J. (April, 1982). "Bowl-A-fact: A game for reviewing the number facts," *Arithmetic Teacher.*

Low

$$1 + 2 + 4 = 7$$
$$2 \times 1 + 4 = 6$$
$$2 \times (1 + 4 = 5$$
$$10 = 1 + 2 + 3 + 4$$
$$1 = 4 - 2 - 1$$
$$7 = 4 + 1 + 2$$
$$3 = 4 - 2 + 1$$
$$6 = 2 + 4 \times 1$$

Did you get a strike? _____

Question 5

Point of View

Suggested time allotment
One class period

Student social organization
Students working individually

Task

Assumed background: This task assumes that starting as early as kindergarten, children have had a variety of experiences with visualization, particularly imagining how something will appear from different points of view. Those experiences will include moving a small number of distinctive objects around on a horizontal surface, observing them from different viewpoints, and describing the relationships among them.

Presenting the task: The teacher should spend a brief period of time in an activity that involves imagining objects from different points of view. Three students (A, B, and C) should stand in the middle of the classroom, while the other children stand around the edges of the room. A, B, and C should be separated from each other by a few feet. Some of the children on the outside then should be asked to describe the order in which they see the three children, from left to right. Mary, for example, might see them as B, A, C, while Altoria, on the opposite side of the room, might see them as C, A, and B. Then everyone (including A, B, and C) should be asked to describe what Manuel, another child on the outside, sees. The teacher can conclude with questions like, "Who are the children who see C in the middle?", "Who sees B directly in front of C?", etc.

Student assessment activity: The teacher should distribute the questions along with the playground map, which is on a separate page. He or she should read the story on the students' sheet as the students read it, being sure that everyone realizes that the story refers to the map. The students will record responses both on the map and on the instruction sheet, so both pieces of paper should be collected at the end.

James has rented a rowboat to row in the pond around the playground. On the playground there are three pieces of equipment:

a play fort:

an umbrella:

and a merry-go-round:

Look at the map. Find James in his boat. Imagine how the playground looks to James. From where James was, the playground looked like this:

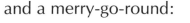

The merry-go-round was on the left, the umbrella was on the right, and the fort was in the middle.

1. James rowed in the pond for a while. When he looked at the playground a second time, this is what it looked like:

Figure out where James was when he saw the playground this way. Draw a dot there and label it **A**.

2. Then James rowed some more. He came to another spot, and stopped. When he looked at the playground from this spot, it looked different. From here, the playground looked like this:

Where was James now? Please draw another dot on the map to show where James was and label it **B**.

3. James really enjoyed rowing, so he rowed some more and explored some more. After a while he was at the spot marked **C**.

Please draw the fort, the umbrella, and the merry-go-round in the space below, to show the way the playground looked to James when he looked at it from the spot marked **C**.

4. It was a warm, pleasant day, and James thought that maybe he would keep on rowing all afternoon. He rowed to a new spot on the pond. When he looked toward the playground, he was suddenly surprised. He could no longer see the umbrella! All he could see was the fort on the left, and the merry-go-round on the right.

Please draw a dot on the map to show where James was when he discovered that he could not see the umbrella. Label it **D**.

5. Do you think that James could row to a spot on the pond where he sees the fort on his left and the umbrella on his right, but he can't see the merry-go-round? _____ Please explain how you know.

Name _____ Date _____

Map of the Playground

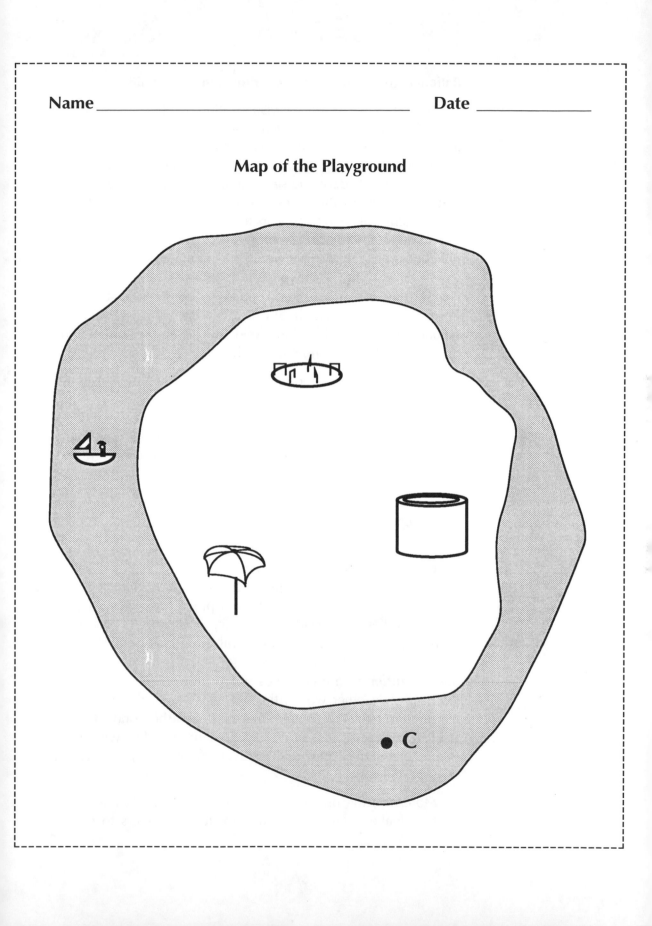

● C

Rationale for the mathematics education community

Studies of the relation of visualization ability to mathematical ability are numerous. At least three issues appear to emerge from these studies. First, there seems to be a rather strong correlation between being good at visualizing and being good at mathematics. (And, of course, in addition to this general correlation, for many mathematics problems visualization is a direct requirement). Second, it appears to be true that improving one's visualization ability after about age 8 or 10 is very difficult, if not impossible. From this it would appear that developing good visualization ability while young is a matter of real importance. Finally, there is evidence that children whose greatest strengths lie in the area of visualization are often poorly served by schools, because these children seldom have any opportunity to make use of this very important skill.

Recognizing the importance of early visualization experiences, other nations (e.g., the Netherlands) include appropriate instruction early in the curriculum. One purpose of including this assessment task in the collection is to encourage such visualization experiences in the curriculum in the first four grades in the U.S.

Task design considerations: Several issues connected with the presentation of this task merit discussion.

First, the task deals only with the relative positions of the three objects — their order from left to right — not the appearance of each individual object. Thus the playground equipment has been chosen so that each piece looks almost the same regardless of the side from which it is viewed. The fort, for example, is a simple cylinder, with no door or other external features that would necessitate taking into account the object's differing appearances when viewed from different directions. In other words, the fort, taken by itself, will look the same to James no matter where he is on the pond. Other standard pieces of playground equipment (a slide, swing set, even a tetherball pole) would look very different to James as he rows around them.

Moreover, the drawings are deliberately simple and stylized, to make them easy enough for fourth graders to copy.

Each piece of equipment is shown in the same size, regardless of James' distance from it.

The pictures of the three objects, as they are drawn on the map, look as if the point of view is somewhere above and to the front of the island, from the reader's perspective. That is, one sees some of the top and some of the side of each. But the pictures of the objects on the student pages are from that same point of view, even though James would not see them that way from his place on the lake. In a sense, then, the representations of the merry-go-round, fort, and umbrella are *symbols* for the objects, rather than realistic pictures of them. (Note, however, that their relative sizes are reasonable.)

This is a standard convention in drawing maps, but it may place a greater burden on some students because they must infer for themselves what these pictures mean. Although James will never see the fort exactly as it is shown in question 1, he will see the three objects in the order shown, and that is what the task is all about.

Why not use very small three-dimensional objects to place on a playground map instead of the symbolic drawings used here? Although the use of such manipulative materials are called for in the *Standards*, there are several advantages to the symbolic drawings. First, the purpose of the assessment is to determine how well children can *imagine* what James' views from particular points on the lake are, in the absence of real objects. Second, the "difficulty" in using symbols for the objects would remain, because the small models are themselves symbols, albeit three-dimensional ones. And third, using three-dimensional models of equipment puts more of a premium on the child's drawing abilities; no longer can he or she simply copy an already-drawn picture or symbol of the object.

Nonetheless, it is worth reiterating that many concrete experiences that involve moving around to get different views of real objects are an essential part of developing visualization abilities. The assumption is that the early years of elementary school will provide many such experiences with small scale objects before students are asked to move to symbolic representations.

Variants and extensions: By adding more pieces of playground equipment or changing their relative positions, many variants of the task can be derived.

Another set of tasks can be created by asking the students to locate pieces of equipment on the playground so that certain views are possible. The teacher would say to the students, "As James rows around on the lake, he can see these views of the playground. Show where the fort, umbrella, merry-go-round, and tree might be so that these views would be possible."

An extension suggested by the discussion of task design considerations above would be to put some identifying marks on the playground equipment so that one or more of the pieces would look different from different directions. For instance, one could put a single access door on the base of the fort.

Protorubric

The pictures below show where the dots for A, B, and D could be placed. See the following pages for additional details.

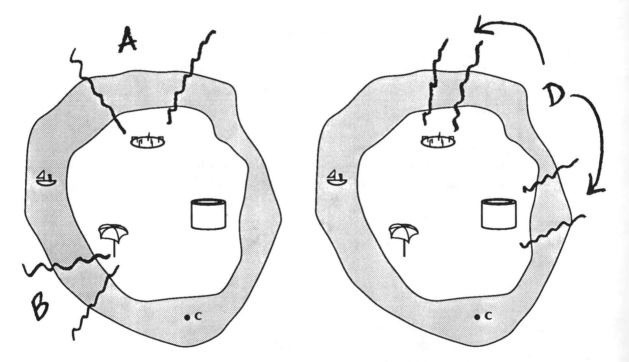

Characteristics of the high response:

The response shows that there is a firm connection between the playground map representation of the situation and the pictures from James' viewpoint.

The dots are all labeled within the limits indicated in the answer key above. (Note that a location for D in which the fort blocks the umbrella is preferable to one in which the merry-go-round blocks the umbrella, because it looks as if the merry-go-round is not tall enough.) The pictures in question 3 are drawn in the correct order, although the individual drawings can be just good enough to be recognizable.

The explanation for question 5 is well reasoned. Ordinarily, in a high response, the child says "No," and explains that if the fort is on the left and the umbrella on the right, then the merry-go-round has to be in front of both of them.

High

> Maybe the merry-go-round is so far to his left that he can't see it. It's like out of his view. All he can see is the fort and the umbrella. And then the fort would be on his left and the umbrella is on his right. The merry-go-round is almost behind him.

Question 5

> No I don't think that's possible. The only thing that's big enough to block the merry-go-round is the fort and if he's where the fort is in front of the MGR then the umbrella is on his left not his right so its not possible.

Question 5

Other high responses will be more inventive: "If the boat is where the view of the merry-go-round is blocked by the fort, then James will see the fort on his left and the umbrella on his right if he stands on his head." An unanticipated response like this shows a mature ability to visualize!

Characteristics of the medium response:

The response shows an overall grasp of the situation; at most, one of the responses to questions 1 through 4 is incorrect.

The response to question 5 is correct, (No), but the explanation is inadequate. For example, "I couldn't find a place where that would happen."

Characteristics of the low response:

> Low
>
> I DON'T KNOW - JAMES SEES 3 THINGS ALL THE TIME. HE ROWS AROUND AND AROUND.
>
> Question 5

There is some understanding of the relationship between the playground map and the views that James sees from various places on the lake, but it is tenuous.

At least one of the answers to questions 1, 2, and 4 are within the bounds specified at the beginning of the protorubric.

References

Clements, Douglas H. and Battista, Michael T. (1992). "Geometry and spatial reasoning" in Grouws, Douglas A (ed.) *Handbook of research on mathematics teaching and learning.* New York: Macmillan.

deLange, Jan (1987). *Mathematics, insight, and meaning.* Utrecht: Rijksuniversiteit Utrecht.

Freudenthal, Hans (1983). *Didactical phenomenology of mathematical structures.* Dordrecht: Reidel.

Piaget, Jean, Inhelder, Barbel, and Szeminska, Alina (1960). *The child's conception of geometry.* New York: Basic Books.

The Quilt Designer

> *Apply modern technology to learning and assessment*
>
> *Use aesthetics in mathematics*
>
> *Broaden the view of mathematics appropriate for 4th grade*
>
> *Use geometry in a visually appealing way*

Suggested time allotment
Three class periods

Student social organization
Students working alone

Task

Assumed background: There are two principal assumptions about the students' preparation. First, children should have had many and varied experiences with manipulating geometric objects to create patterns of various kinds. This includes experience with geometric transformations and symmetries. Second, since the computer software around which the task is built runs on Macintosh computers, the students should be familiar with the standard conventions that are typical of Macintosh programs.

A third assumption is that there are as many computers available as there are students who are being assessed at any one time.

Presenting the task: The teacher describes a software package that enables users to design quilts on the computer. Giving each student a handout showing the screens below, the teacher should guide the group through the first example of a sequence of designs, with students using their own computers to reproduce the example. Note: a limited number of copies of the Quilt Designer software are available for $20 (prepaid) by writing to MSEB, 2101 Constitution Avenue, NW, HA 476, Washington, DC 20418.

Essentially, the Quilt Designer program allows a child to create a "quilt" of 64 squares by starting with a basic square of his or her own design. This starting square is acted upon by a sequence of three 2 X 2 designs, each entry of which is a rotation through 0°, 90°, 180°, or 270°. Thus the initial basic square design becomes a 2 X 2 quilt, each square of which is a congruent (and perhaps rotated) copy of the initial design; the rotations are specified by the first pattern of arrows. The second pattern of arrows turns that into a 4 X 4 quilt, and the third pattern of arrows results in an 8 X 8 quilt.

When the Quilt Designer program starts, the user can retrieve work that is already in progress, or start a new quilt. In the latter case, the first screen that appears allows one to design the basic unit square.

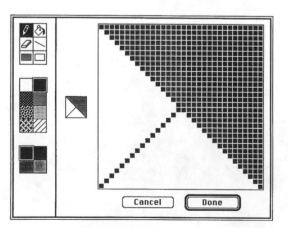

The Quilt Designer

The space on the right is reserved for a greatly expanded picture of the unit square, which can be designed pixel by pixel. The tools shown along the left edge of the screen are the standard Macintosh drawing tools — the pencil (for changing individual pixels), the paint bucket (for filling in entire areas), the eraser, the line-draw tool, and two kinds of rectangle-drawing options, filled and unfilled. Various kinds of shading are also available. Another option superimposes a rectangular grid as an aid to drawing.

Once the child has created a unit square, he clicks "Done"; the program immediately goes to the screen on which the quilt will now be built. The unit square that was just created is reproduced on this screen, along with three sets of arrows. Initially, all the arrows are pointing up, as in the figure below.

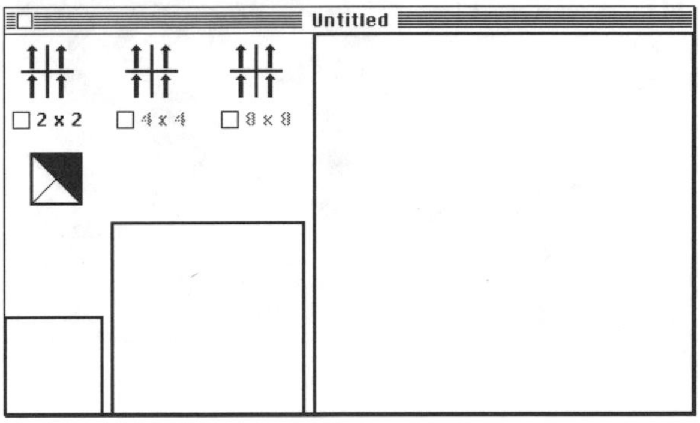

The user can click on any arrow at any time; each click rotates the arrow 90° counterclockwise. When the child wants to construct the 2 X 2 design, he clicks on the box under the first configuration of arrows. Immediately the 2 X 2 pattern is created.

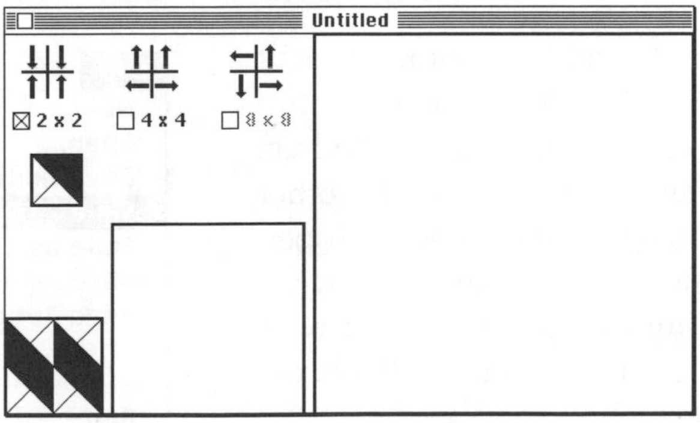

The 4 X 4 designs and the final 8 X 8 quilt are created in a similar way, each building on its predecessor, as shown below.

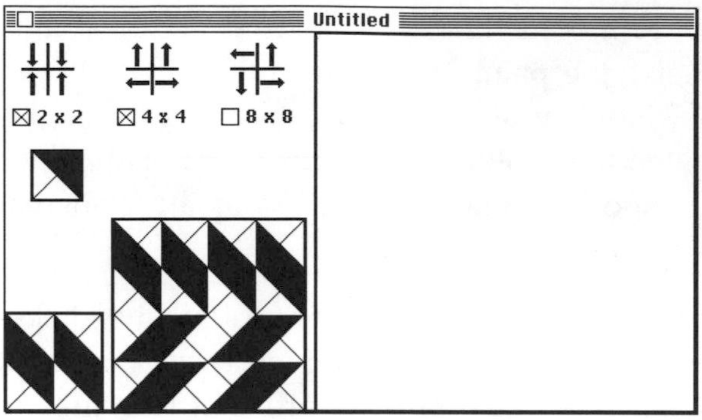

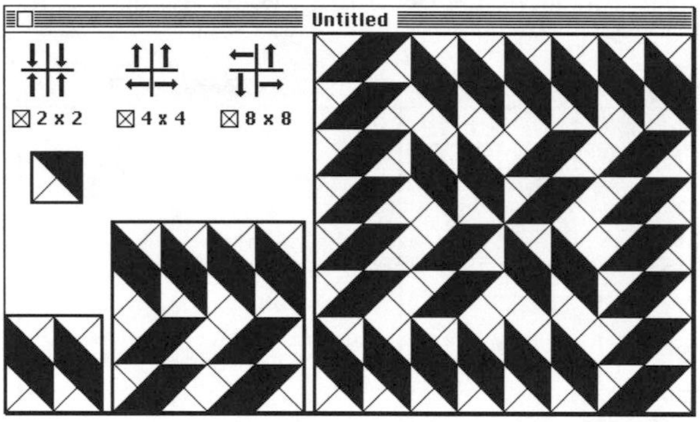

Even after the 8 X 8 design has been completed, the user can change any or all of the arrows that specified the rotations. All the drawings that are affected are instantly updated, so that the effects of different patterns of rotations can be seen quickly. The user can also edit the unit square itself and see the effects on whatever designs (2 X 2, 4 X 4, or 8 X 8) have been created so far.

Once the quilt is completed, it can be saved under a name chosen by the user. This is accomplished via a pull-down menu. Using the other options from the menu, one can open two (or more) quilts at the same time, so that one can be compared with another. A "Print" option allows the quilt to be printed on paper.

Student assessment activity: A suggested schedule for the assessment tasks is outlined below.

Days 1 and 2: Students are given the opportunity to explore other examples on their own. The teacher should encourage students to experiment with positions of the arrows and to try to predict how a change in a single arrow will affect the appearance of the 8 X 8 quilt. This is complicated, because the effect will depend not only on the symmetries (if any) of the unit square itself, but also on the positions of arrows in a preceding pattern.

Similarly, students should be encouraged to experiment with changing the order of the arrows. For example, the teacher could say: "For what kinds of unit squares will these two sets of arrows produce the same final quilt?"

Another set of investigations involves working backwards. The teacher could ask: "Given a final 8 X 8 quilt (which the teacher can create and print out), what initial unit square and three arrow patterns could have produced it?" "Is there more than one possibility for any of them?"

Day 3: Students are asked to write a description of their *favorite* quilt, explain what features make it especially attractive or interesting, and then describe how they went about creating it.

Name _____ **Date** _____

Of all the quilts you have made so far, which one is your favorite? Write its file name here: _____. Also PRINT it, and attach it to this paper.

1. Why do you especially like this quilt?   What features or parts of the design make it interesting, or attractive, or unusual?

2. Please explain as well as you can the steps that you went through to create this quilt. What did you start with? How did you decide what to do next?

Rationale for the mathematics education community

The Quilt Designer task has some unusual features that distinguish it from some of the other tasks in this collection: (a) it illustrates connections between mathematics and another discipline — in this case, art; (b) it allows children to express their own creativity in a way that is not ordinarily associated with the study of mathematics — in part, students decide what is "right" based on their own aesthetic sense; and (c) it uses modern technology and sophisticated software to enable students to explore mathematical concepts heretofore inaccessible through traditional means. A related issue for tomorrow's mathematics students is how well and how quickly they can learn to use novel computer programs flexibly and effectively.

Moreover, the task incorporates important mathematical skills (e.g., prediction, spatial visualization) and concepts (e.g., symmetry, rigid transformations, the composite of two transformations) that are not often seen in the fourth grade curriculum. In the process, it gently introduces some fundamental algebraic and geometric ideas.

The Quilt Designer has potential as an extended classroom activity as well. The choice of a favorite quilt does not require a strictly mathematical explanation (see the protorubric section). However, with additional classroom time spent with the program, instructional questions could be posed to students to motivate them toward *mathematically* interesting reasons for preferring a design.

The Quilt Designer program, in fact, captured the imagination of many students in the pilot; they asked that the software be made available for future experimentation.

Task design considerations: The assessment task suggested here for Day 3 (as well as the introductory activities) emphasize the children's aesthetic sense, their abilities to use the software to create designs or patterns that they find interesting or appealing, and their abilities to explain what they have done and why. Clearly one could ask questions that more narrowly focus on particular skills or abilities, but one of the purposes of including the Quilt Designer is to illustrate assessment tasks that are more open-ended and creative.

In situations in which many Macintosh computers are tied together into a local area network, the child might fill out the assessment sheet electronically. In that case the quilt would not be printed out on paper at all; the teacher (or other assessor) would simply access the file that the child designated.

Design of the software. Whenever questions of style arose in the programming of The Quilt Designer, the standard conventions of Macintosh programming were used (even though in some cases it might have been desirable to alter them a bit). As a result, anyone who is familiar with other Macintosh applications will find the mechanics of The Quilt Designer to be perfectly straightforward; and if The Quilt Designer is someone's first experience with Macintosh computers, it will not interfere with subsequent encounters with Macintosh programs.

One important design question as the software was written was what symbol to use in the patterns of arrows. This version of the program uses an arrow pointing straight up, to the left, down, and to the right; this is intended to be reminiscent of a pointer on a dial. The arrow shows the result of the rotation, not the rotation itself. While an advantage of the dial-pointer notation is that it helps in visualizing the effects of a rotation on a given unit square, a disadvantage is that it will no longer be usable if reflections are used in addition to rotations. (See the discussion of extensions of the Quilt Designer, below.)

Variants and extensions: As suggested above, there are many variants of assessment tasks that would tap more explicitly and directly the child's ability to visualize the geometric transformations involved in creating quilts. For example, at a very basic level, one could give the child the 4 X 4 stage of a quilt, together with the final quilt, and ask what final pattern of arrows would produce it. If the 4 X 4 design, as a whole, has axes of symmetry there will be more than one set of arrows that will give the final quilt.

A natural extension of the Quilt Designer would be to allow reflections ("flips") as well as rotations. This would necessitate eight distinct symbols; one for each of the eight rigid motions of the square into itself. One would have to experiment to see if symbols that suggest the results of the transformations would be more or less easily understood than symbols that suggest the transformations themselves.

Protorubric

Note that the descriptions of the high, medium, and low responses below pertain to all three days of the Quilt Designer activity, not just to the final responses about the "favorite quilt."

Characteristics of the high response:

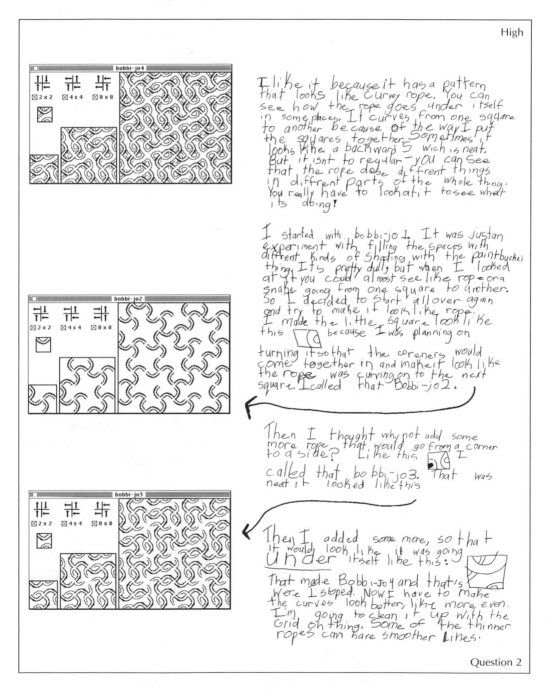

High

I like it because it has a pattern that looks like curvey rope. You can see how the rope goes under itself in some places. It curves from one square to another because of the way I put the squares together. Sometimes it looks like a backward S wich is neat. But it isnt to regular—you can see that the rope does diffrent things in diffrent parts of the whole thing. You really have to look at it to see what its doing!

I started with bobbi-jo 1. It was just an experiment with filling the spaces with diffrent kinds of shading with the paintbuckei thing. It's pretty dull, but when I looked at it you could almost see like rope ona snake going from one square to another. So I decided to start all over again and try to make it look like rope. I made the little square look like this because I was planning on turning it so that the coreners would come together in and make it look like the rope was curving on to the next square. I called that Bobbi-jo2.

Then I thought why not add some more rope, that would go from a corner to a side? Like this. I called that bobbi-jo3. That was neat it looked like this

Then I added some more, so that it would look like it was going under itself like this:
That made Bobbi-jo4 and that's were I stoped. Now I have to make the curves look better, like more even. I'm going to clean it up with the grid on thing. Some of the thinner ropes can have smoother lines.

Question 2

The child explores the software productively, creating interesting patterns. Trial-and-error is used systematically to see how changing the initial design and the rotations in the arrows affect the final quilt. The effects of varying the order in which the arrows are used are explored, and the child keeps track of intermediate results in a sensible way (by saving files appropriately). The child can explain clearly why or how the final "favorite quilt" is attractive and how it was produced.

Characteristics of the medium response:

The child understands how the software operates and can create interesting quilts with it. There is not, however, a systematic approach used in exploring the effects on the final quilt of individual changes in the arrows. The idea of working backwards is difficult, and often the predicted arrows do not produce the desired result. The explanations of why the final quilt is interesting and the steps that were used to create it are not completely clear.

Characteristics of the low response:

The child can make quilts using the software, but they are more the result of random trials than any sort of thoughtful planning. Intermediate results are not recorded in any systematic way, so that comparisons of quilts made with the same arrows in different orders, for example, cannot be made. The final quilt of Day 3 shows little sense of balance or form.

Reference

Children's Computer Workshop (formerly a component of Children's Television Workshop) developed a version of this software to run on a Commodore 64 computer.

How Many Buttons?

Suggested time allotment
A total of two or three class periods (one class period of introductory work plus one or two class periods of student work)

Student social organization
Students working in groups of two or three

Task

Assumed background: This task assumes that the children have had experience in gathering data and making estimates in relatively complex situations.

Presenting the task: This assessment is embedded in a context-setting activity introduced by the teacher to the whole class. The context-setting activity takes one class period, and the paired work—the assessment task itself—requires a second class period, possibly spilling over into part of a third.

The following is written as directions to the teacher:

Introduce the activity by telling the students they will be working on estimating the number of buttons *in their class* today.

Ask students for their estimates of the number of buttons in the class. Give students a few minutes to look around—at their own buttons, at the number of buttons that students near them have—and to discuss their estimates with students near them. Collect some of their estimates and list them on the board.

As students are estimating, some questions and issues will probably arise. Encourage students to talk about any questions that occur to them (for example, "What about buttons on sweaters or coats hanging in the closet?" "Were there buttons that they didn't notice or forgot about because they were not in obvious places?" "Should the teacher's buttons be included?" The answers to these questions, which can be decided jointly by you and your students, will depend on your particular situation. For instance, if students' outerwear is stored in an inconvenient location you might decide not to include it.)

Now each student should carefully count the number of buttons that he or she has. They might work in pairs or threes to help each other count carefully. Record their data on a line plot so that everyone in the class can see it. For example:

```
                              X
  X         X   X   X         X
  X         X   X   X         X           X
  X   X     X   X   X   X     X       X               X
_____
  0   1     2   3   4   5     6   7   8   9   10  11  12
```

Encourage students to describe these data by asking: "What would you say about the number of buttons in our class?" Students may comment on the range of the data, where data are clumped, for which values there are no people with exactly that number of buttons, and what (if anything) seems typical of their class.

Student assessment activity: The assessment should be done on the day after the activity just described. You will need the class data from the previous day, and pencil and paper for each student. Of course, they should have access to calculators.

Tell students they will be working in small groups to estimate the number of buttons there are in the whole school. They can refer to the class data from the previous session. Suggest that they may want to consider questions such as: "Is it likely that other classes in the school will have a similar number of buttons?" "Do younger students have fewer or more buttons?" "What about older students?" "How should teachers or other adults in the school be included in the estimate?" These questions should be written on the board. They can contribute greatly to the depth and sophistication of the children's responses, so students should have equal access to them.

Each pair of students then works together to solve this problem, as described above. They should be encouraged to record their strategies, including the numbers they chose and why they chose them.

Rationale for the mathematics education community

This item pushes the curriculum to include work with large numbers and with a complex situation in which estimation is a *legitimate* mathematical process—not simply a prelude to finding the "real" answer. Further, it connects a range of mathematical ideas—multiplicative relationships (e.g., an average of about 6 buttons per student, with 22 students per classroom), estimation, averages ("I decided there are about 22 students in each classroom."), and beginning ideas about sampling. Use of the calculator is incorporated in a natural way.

The problem is accessible: Almost any child can arrive at some solution, but the possible solutions span a broad spectrum of depth and complexity. The problem provides all students with the opportunity to think about and discuss which factors to take into account — whether or not to include adults' buttons or clothes in the closet, and so forth. One strength of a task like this is that its context is immediate and tangible.

Many estimation tasks arise in some setting that provides a "real-life" motivation and a criterion for judging how precise an estimate should be. One must remember, however, that fourth graders are not as concerned as adults are with the "real" reasons for doing something. In this case, classroom trials have suggested that just the allure of the large numbers, of finding out something that no one has ever known before, and of getting the best possible estimate, are plenty of motivation.

The mode of presentation embeds the assessment task as an integral part of a piece of curriculum. Indeed, teachers might want to move from the assessment task back into curriculum by continuing the investigation with the whole class—comparing the students' individual estimates, gathering additional information, and refining these estimates. (See the Variants and extensions section below.)

Finally, it offers a problem on which students work in pairs. Working together to pool information and expertise to come to a solution are essential problem-solving skills for today's students.

Task design considerations: The protorubric for this task is phrased in terms of the factors that the child's response takes into account. Nonetheless, careful consideration must be given to the specific details of the task if it is to be used to make comparisons among, or to draw conclusions about, different kinds of schools in different geographical areas of the country. Depending on the season, a child in a colder climate is likely to wear more clothes, with more buttons, than one from a warmer climate. A school that contains 25 classrooms is a very different setting from one that has five classrooms. Because of such potential variations in complexity, the task would be inappropriate to use universally for comparative purposes.

Variants and extensions: Objects other than buttons can be used in this sort of activity — for example, books that the student happens to have in his or her desk. In fact, this might alleviate (but not eliminate) some of the geographical differences noted above.

Using the task as the basis for extended classroom discussion might be particularly valuable. One can continue the investigation by considering how many buttons there might be in all the schools in the town or city, or even all the schools in the state. This would involve the use of almanacs or atlases to find out the appropriate numbers to use, depending on the question. Similarly, students might explore how the number of buttons that people wear varies from one section of the country to another. Thus, the students would want to communicate with at least one other school of the same size in some other region and compare data.

Protorubric

Characteristics of the high response:

The response appropriately takes into consideration the following aspects of the problem: (a) the data collected from the day before; (b) some estimate of the number of children per classroom; (c) the number of classes in the school; (d) variation of buttons among children of various ages; and (e) adults' buttons (which the pair may choose to disregard entirely).

High

There are four rooms of each grade and 6 grades 4×6 =24. And there is afternoon Kindergarden and morning kindergarden 2 each and so thats 28 classes! On Friday we found there were 63 buttons in our room! We didn't count Mrs. Sorenson's buttons, or anybodys Campane buttons. Little kids don't have as many buttons so we thought maybe 50 a class for 1frist and second grades and kindergarden. So we ~~dit~~ multiplied 50 times 12 that's 600 and 63 times 16 that's 1008 and we said 1000. Then we added and got 1600 which is our answer. It may not be exactly right. You may want to lessen that because the morning and afternoon kindergarden kids arn't in school at the same time. So you would subtract 100 that would be 1500.

Reasonable justifications are given for how each numerical value was chosen or calculated.

The numerical values are put together with appropriate arithmetic processes. (For example, if the students decided there were an average of 90 buttons in each of the 12 upper grade classrooms and an average of 60 buttons in each of the 8 lower grade classrooms, they would calculate with these values so that their result would be (90 x 12) + (60 x 8), not in some invalid way, such as adding 90 and 60, then multiplying by the total number of classrooms.)

The final report on the solution clearly details the steps the students went through to solve the problem so that a reader can easily follow their solution strategy.

Characteristics of the medium response:

Medium

Yesterday we found our class had 27 buttons in our class. We think there are 11 classrooms in Baxter and so we did 27 eleven times.

$$\begin{array}{r} 27 \\ \times 11 \\ \hline 27 \\ 27 \\ \hline 297 \end{array}$$

That's 297 buttons in all.

The end

The response takes into consideration the results of the previous day's work. Further, it uses a reasonable estimate for the number of students per class (if needed for the solution) and the number of classrooms in the school, with appropriate justifications for the values chosen.

Consideration of factors like variation of button numbers by age of child or adults' buttons is lacking.

The arithmetic processes are appropriate.

The final report on the solution clearly explains some (but not all) aspects of the student's strategy.

Characteristics of the low response:

Low

There are thirty-eight buttons in our class. There are 24 kids in our class. There are 7 classes in our school. We multiplied with a calculater. We got 6384.

Some reference is made to the previous day's work, and some other values may be chosen reasonably.

Either some values (e.g., the number of students per class or the number of classes) are chosen inappropriately, or the way in which the arithmetic processes are used is incorrect.

The explanation and justification of the student's reasoning is incomplete or unclear.

Reference

"Investigations in Number, Data, and Space" project of TERC, Cambridge, MA.

The Taxman

Suggested time allotment
One class period

Student social organization
Working alone or in pairs, following a videotaped introduction

Task

Assumed background: This task assumes that children are familiar with the concept of factors of whole numbers and, in particular, with prime numbers. It also assumes that they have had some experience in developing multi-step strategies and in articulating those strategies coherently.

Presenting the task: The problem is to analyze a game that we assume is unfamiliar to the children. Hence the first task for the teacher is to introduce the rules of the game. One way of doing this is to show a videotape in which a teacher shows a small group of

> *Develop strategies based on systematic analysis*
>
> *Present convincing arguments*
>
> *Use uniform introduction for all classes*
>
> *Generalize from specific cases*

children how the game of Taxman is played. The script for such a videotape is given below. (If a tape is not available, the classroom teacher can use the script as a guide to introducing the game.)

The scene opens in a classroom setting, with a teacher and a group of six students. There is a chalkboard on one wall.

Teacher: Today I'm going to show you how to play a new number game, called Taxman. The game is played with a list of numbers starting with the number one. For example, the Taxman game with six numbers would start with this list: [Teacher writes list on chalkboard]

1   2   3   4   5   6

There are two players, You and the Taxman. Every time it is your turn, you can take any number in the list, as long as at least some factors of that number are also in the list. You get your number, and the Taxman gets all of the factors of that number that are in the list. For example, if you take 4, . . .

Student A: . . . then the Taxman would get 2!

Teacher: Why?

Student A: Because 2 is a factor of 4.

Student B: The Taxman'd get 1, too.

Student C: Oh, yeah, because 1's a factor of 4.

Teacher: So if you took 4, then the list would look like this: [writes]

1̸   2̸   3   4̸   5   6

Now you have 4 points . . .

Student D: . . . and the Taxman has 3 points. [Teacher writes]

You	Taxman
4	**2**
	1

The Taxman

Teacher: So, the first rule of the Taxman game is:

1. The Taxman *must* get something every time.

That means you can't choose if there aren't any factors of that number still in the list. The only other rule is this:

2. When none of the numbers in the list has any factors left in the list, then the game is over, and the Taxman gets all the numbers that are left in the list.

Student E: I don't get the second rule.

Teacher: Let's play a game together to see what this second rule means. We'll use the same list:

1	**2**	**3**	**4**	**5**	**6**

What would you like to start with?

Student F: 6. [Teacher gives chalk to Student F, who crosses off the "6" and records 6 points for You.]

1	**2**	**3**	**4**	**5**	**6̸**

You
6

Student A: So the Taxman gets 3 and 2 [crosses them off the list] . . .

Student B: . . . and 1 [crosses off 1 and updates the score].

1̸	**2̸**	**3̸**	**4**	**5**	**6̸**

You   **Taxman**
6   **3**
                      2
                      1

Student F: So now you could take 5.

Student E: No you can't! 5 doesn't have any factors that are left on the list.

Student F: Oh, OK. The 1's not there any more. How about 4?

Student D: That won't work either. The factors of 4 are 1 and 2, and they're both gone already.

Student F: Oh, I see. So the game is over?

Teacher: Right. At this point, the only the numbers left are 4 and 5. Neither of these has any factors that are still in the list. So the game is over, and the Taxman gets both the 4 and the 5: [writes]

1 2 3 4 5 6

You	Taxman
6	3
	2
	1
	5
	4
	15

Student C: So You lost — 6 to 15.

Student B: I bet we can do better than that.

Teacher: Well, let's see. We'll start with our list again: [writes]

1 2 3 4 5 6

Student F: How about if we start with 5 this time? [Student F crosses off the 5]

Student B: Hah! The Taxman only gets 1. [Crosses off 1 and records scores]

1 2 3 4 5 6

You	Taxman
5	1

Student A: Now take 6.

Student D: No, wait a minute. If you do that, the Taxman'll get 3 and 2.

Student E: And then you won't be able to take the 4 . . .

Student D: . . . 'cause the 2 and 1'll be gone.

Student A: So take the 4 now.

Student C: Yeah, that'd be better. Then the Taxman'll get only the 2.

Student F: And you'll still be able to take the 6.

Teacher: Wait a second. I don't follow you. So what do you want to do now?

Student B: Take the 4, so the Taxman gets the 2. [Crosses off and records scores.]

1̶	2̶	3	4̶	5̶	6

	You	**Taxman**
	5	1
	4	2

Student E: And now you can choose the 6 because the 3 is still left for the Taxman. [Crosses off and records scores.]

1̶	2̶	3̶	4̶	5̶	6̶

	You	**Taxman**
	5	1
	4	2
	6	3
	15	**6**

Student D: So this time, You won, 15 to 6!

Teacher: Do you think you could ever do better, starting with the list from 1 to 6?

Student A: I don't think so. . . .

Student C: I'm positive there's no way to do any better than that.

Teacher: How do you know?

Student C: Well, look. Every time you play, the Taxman has to get something, right? So that means...

(Fade to black)

Following the viewing of the videotape, let students play a game of Taxman using more than six numbers. In small groups they can play Taxman-8:

1   2   3   4   5   6   7   8

Together the group should choose the numbers to claim for You; then one student removes that number and updates the score, while another member of the group removes the factors and updates the Taxman's score. Remind the students that the Taxman *must always get something.*

Student assessment activity: See the following pages. A Spanish translation is provided after the English version.

Play several games of Taxman with these ten numbers:

1   2   3   4   5   6   7   8   9   10

Make a record of your best game. Be sure to show which numbers you took and the order in which you took them, not just the final score.

Then answer the following questions:

1. Did you beat the Taxman? _____

2. What number did you choose first? _____ Why?

3. Do you think anyone could ever play a better game than your best game? _____ Explain why or why not.

4. Suppose you were going to play Taxman with the whole numbers from 1 to 95. What number would you choose first? _____ Why?

Nombre _____ **Fecha** _____

Juega varios partidos de el Cobrador de Impuestos con estos diez números:

1   2   3   4   5   6   7   8   9   10

Mantín un registro de tu mejor partido. Asegúrate de escribir los números que escogiste y en el orden en que los escogiste, y no solamente tu puntuación final.

A medida que investigas el juego de el Cobrador de Impuestos con los diez números, contesta las siguientes preguntas:

1. ¿Puedes ganarle al cobrador de impuestos? _____

2. ¿Qué número escogerías primero? _____ ¿Por qué?

3. ¿Crees que alguien pudiera jugar un partido mejor que el tuyo? Explica por qué sí o por qué no.

4. Imaginate que vas a jugar al Cobrador de Impuestos con los números del 1 al 95. ¿Qué número escogerías primero? _____ ¿Por qué?

Rationale for the mathematics education community

The Taxman task provides a good example of a mathematical situation in which systematic analysis involving several steps is critical, an important characteristic of mathematical power. The task also presents an opportunity for children to generalize what they have learned beyond the particular instance; e.g. analyzing Taxman-10 to describe a strategy for Taxman-95. At the same time, the task asks students to construct convincing arguments about their strategy. These steps are all essential facets of mathematical proofs.

Moreover, the task is a situation in which reasoning with prime numbers, composites, and factors plays a vital role; it is up to the children, however, to determine how these ideas should be applied to analyzing the game.

It is worth noting that the Taxman game has no pretense of applications to the "real world" in the usual sense; it is a purely abstract, without grounding in some physical context. But games are a significant aspect of a fourth grader's real world and can be motivational in and of themselves.

To ensure that children from different classrooms will get exactly the same introduction to the game, the use of a video-taped introduction is recommended. Uniformity of presentation is important if the results of one classroom are to be compared fairly with results from another. The widespread availability of videocassette recorders in classrooms now makes it feasible to introduce problem settings that would previously have been too complex to replicate reliably from one classroom to another.

Certain features of the Taxman task — and other potential assessment tasks — make a uniform introduction even more important. With a videotape, everyone will have the same experiences in exploring optimal and non-optimal choices. A teacher who introduces the games in his or her classroom without the videotape might never consider an opening move of 6, for example, simply because no one in the class happened to offer it as a choice during the explanation.

Task design considerations: A few points about the construction of this task should be made:

First, the choice of the number 95 for the last question was made very carefully. One would expect even a fairly unsophisticated child to recognize that 95 is a multiple of 5, and therefore not prime; it is also straightforward to recognize 93 as being composite — a multiple of 3. It's harder to see that 91 is also not a prime, and that in fact the largest available prime (and therefore one's best first move) is 89. Hence the choice of Taxman-95 can yield information about the child's conceptions of primes and factors that other games would not necessarily reveal. (Suppose instead that the task had been to choose the best first number in Taxman-101. If a child (correctly) chose 101 one could not determine whether she chose it because it was a large prime, a large odd number, or just large.)

Related to this point, in a pilot, an earlier version of this task asked, "Did you find any strategies that might be useful if you were playing Taxman with some other set of numbers? If you did, please explain." Clearly this is much more open-ended than the current version. Since the point was to see if the child understands the role of prime numbers in Taxman, the last question was narrowed down so that it addressed more specifically the strategy for finding an optimal first move.

Second, the instruction to "Play several games of Taxman . . . ." is similar to instructions in some of the other prototypes (see, for example, the Hog Game task). The wording is intermediate between specifying exactly how many games should be played, on the one hand, and, on the other, not saying anything at all about playing the game. It is left up to the child to determine (a) how many games to play, (b) how (if at all) to record them. Knowing how much experimentation is needed or when enough data is available are important features of mathematical power. Clearly a decision about how much direction to provide through the instructions is a matter of judgment for the task designer. Presumably older students would be in a better position to determine if they need to play any games at all.

Note also the wording near the beginning of the task: "Make a record of your best game," rather than "Make a record of each game." The latter instruction tells students what to do, while the former lets them decide for themselves what they need to do. The NCTM *Standards* call for students who can make cogent decisions in the problem-solving process.

Third, question 3 is phrased "Do you think *anyone* could play a better game . . .?" rather than "Do you think *you* could play a better game . . . ?" to encourage children to create a proof. In effect, the student is being asked to complete the argument that Student C started as the videotape fades out: According to the rules, the Taxman must get at least one number for every number that You claims. So if there are 10 numbers in all, the Taxman must get at least 5 of them. Further, it is possible to play the game (by You choosing 7, 9, 6, 8, and 10, in that order) so that the Taxman gets only five numbers, and they are the smallest five. Hence there is no better game. Question 4 also calls for a short proof: The Taxman is going to get the number 1 as the result of the first move (no matter what it is), and hence no prime number can be chosen after the first move. Therefore, one might as well choose a prime on the first move, and, in fact, the largest prime available. Since 89 is the largest prime less than 95, 89 is the best first move.

A related point: One should be aware that there may be cultural or personality effects operating in question 3. Some children will think that it is generally unseemly or boastful to claim that anything they do is "best." Others may think that it is important to put up a front of asserting that whatever they do is "best." Or perhaps prior personal experiences have convinced the child that nothing he or she does could be "best." Thus the answers given to question 3 may depend on factors other than those that are really relevant to the mathematics. Part of the point of developing one's reasoning abilities, however, is to become better able to distinguish between "the best possible" from "the best that I personally can do."

Note that Taxman with larger numbers is much harder to analyze when one gets beyond the first few moves.

The general points about the translation into Spanish that appear in the discussion of the Checkers Tournament task apply here as well.

Variants and extensions: One natural variant of the task is to use different sets of numbers — from 1 through 15, for example, or 1 through 20. (One should keep in mind the earlier caveat that complete analyses of the games become considerably harder as the numbers increase.)

Another variation of the same kind is to replace 95 (in question 4) with a smaller number, keeping in mind the points made above about how 95 was chosen.

Of course the numbers do not have to be consecutive whole numbers starting with 1. What happens if the numbers are the odd numbers from 1 through 19, or the even numbers from 2 through 20?

Another possibility is to concentrate more on the number theoretical ideas than the sequencing of moves, by looking at the score after only one move. Consider Taxman-65, for example (starting with the set of whole numbers from 1 through 65). A starting move of 62 means that You leads, 62 to 34 (which is 31 + 2 + 1). A starting move of 60, on the other hand would put You behind, 60 to 108 (which is the sum of all the other factors of 60). An opening move of 6 would result in a tie, 6 to 6. The following questions would be of interest: "Which opening moves result in You leading, which result in the Taxman leading, and which result in a tie? Are there opening moves that result in scores for You and the Taxman that differ by just one point? What are the underlying patterns here?"

Protorubric

Characteristics of the high response:

The high-level response is one that demonstrates an optimal game, communicates it effectively, and, generally shows an understanding of choosing the largest available prime as the best first move.

In response to the questions about Taxman-10, the pair of students present a winning game with

---

High

Nobody could because I got the 5 highest numbers 7, 9, 6, 8 & 10 = 40 He got the lowest 5 numbers.

Question 3

Do 89 first because the only thing that goes into 89 is 1, and 89 is the biggest number thats like that. Anything you do the taxman will get 1

Question 4

the optimal score, in a form that can be followed clearly. For example, this table is given:

You	Taxman
7	1
9	3
6	2
8	4
10	5
40	15

The first number chosen, 7, is justified on the basis that it is the largest prime on the list, or on a basis that amounts to a complete analysis of the game (e.g., "I chose the 7 first because if I chose the 10, then . . .; and if I chose the 9, then . . .; and if I chose the 8, then . . . .").

No better game is possible because "You" has captured the five largest numbers on the list, while giving the Taxman the five smallest numbers.

For the game of Taxman-95, 89 is chosen as the first move. The justification asserts that if any prime is to be chosen at any point in the game, it must be on the first turn. Since 89 is the largest prime number in the list, it's the best first move.

A somewhat less advanced response is simply that 89 is the largest number on the list that has only one factor on the list.

An even less satisfactory response is to declare that the largest prime is the optimal opening move, but then to misidentify 91, 93, or 95 as a prime.

Characteristics of the medium response:

A winning game is described, although it need not be an optimal one.

The first number chosen is justified simply on the basis that it works out to be a winning first move.

A correct answer, with some justification, is given to Question 3. (Of course, this response will have

> Medium
>
> I think I'd do 93 first becasue Taxman gets 3 and 1. 3 and 1 are little numbers and 93 is pretty big.
>
> Question 4

to depend on the best game that the students can find. If a less-than-optimal game is described, then an answer of "Yes" is correct here.)

Some number other than 89 is suggested as the first move, with a rationale that includes some reference to the number's factors. For example, "95, because it's big, and the Taxman would get only 5, 19, and 1."

Characteristics of the low response:

Low

> Yes, because I'm not that good at this game but I tried my hardest.

Question 3

Some game is described, but sketchily and perhaps ambiguously (that is, it may not be possible to tell in what order the numbers were selected).

No justification is provided for the first number chosen, or the justification does not take into account the factors of the number.

In question 4, no reference is made to factors of the number selected as the first move. For example: "95, because it is the biggest number you can get."

Lightning Strikes Again!

> *Use more than one branch of mathematics in problem-solving*
>
> *Apply proportional thinking to real-life experiences*
>
> *Choose tools to help in problem-solving*

Suggested time allotment
One class period

Student social organization
Students working alone

Task

Assumed background: This task assumes that children have had experience in solving complex problems that are posed in the context of a map. In particular, they should have used rulers to measure distances on a map and dealt with converting from map distances to real distances. The task also assumes some familiarity with the use of a compass to find all points that are a particular distance from a given point.

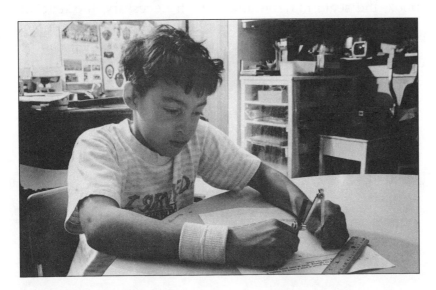

Presenting the task: Each child should have access to drawing tools (pencils, a compass, a ruler). Before passing out the student activity materials, the teacher should conduct a short discussion of lightning, focusing especially on the fact that often you see the flash of lightning before you hear the thunder clap. (Children will probably relate their own experiences of seeing a flash before hearing the rumble.) He or she should explain that the two occur simultaneously, but sound travels more slowly than light. Hence, the thunder is heard after the lightning is seen. In fact, the farther away one is from the flash, the greater is the gap between seeing and hearing. The teacher should describe one way to estimate the distance between someone and a lightning flash: Count the number of seconds between the flash and the thunderclap. That number, divided by five, is approximately the number of miles between the person and the lightning.

The teacher also can discuss safety-related issues as appropriate.

Student assessment activity: The teacher should pass out the student sheets and read the introduction as the class follows along. Discuss questions 1 and 2 as a group to be sure that the students understand the general concepts involved. The students should select tools (ruler, compass, calculator) that are appropriate to the task as they need them.

Note: if the student materials are duplicated from this book, the scale may be affected. If necessary, the teacher should redraw the figure ensuring that the distance from point E to point B on the map is 2 inches. The same map can be used without the lightning in questions 5 through 8.

Name _____ **Date** _____

One way to estimate the distance from you to where lightning strikes is to count the number of seconds until you hear the thunder, and then divide by five. The number you get is the approximate distance in miles.

People are standing at the four points A, B, C and D. They saw lightning strike at point E. Because sound travels more slowly than light, they did not hear the thunder right away.

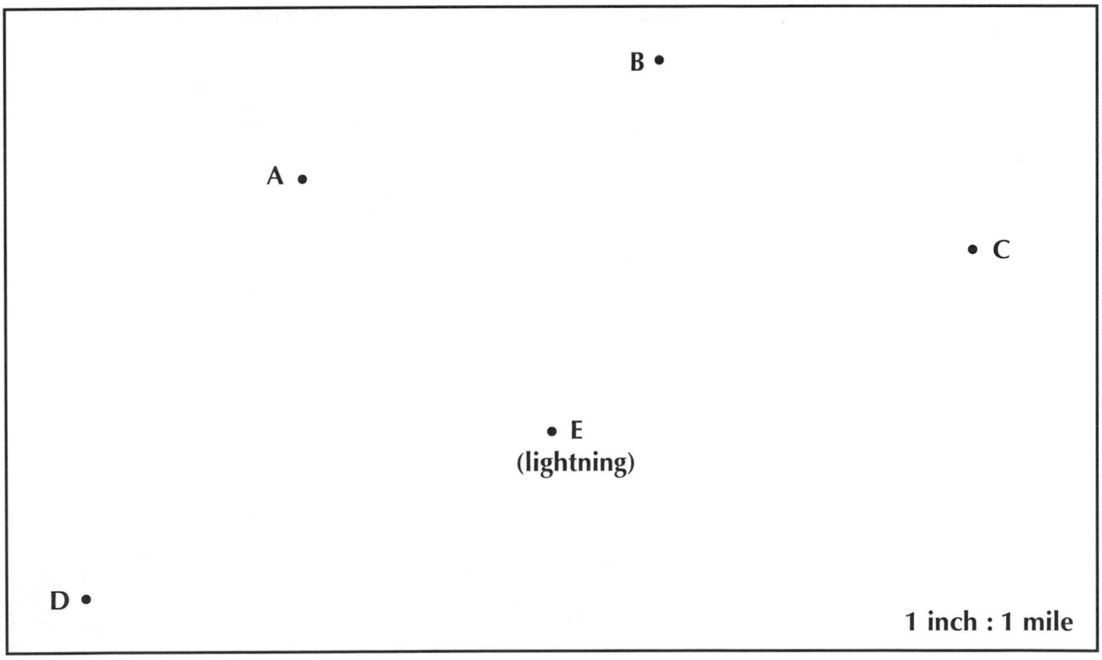

B •

A •

• C

• E
(lightning)

D •

1 inch : 1 mile

1. Who heard the thunder first? _____ Why?

2. Who heard it last? _____ Why?

3. One of the people heard it after 12 seconds. Who was it? _____
Explain your answer.

4. After how many seconds did the person at B hear the thunder? _____
Show how you know.

5. Now suppose lightning strikes again at a <u>different</u> place. The person
at A and the person at C both hear the thunder after the same amount
of time. Show on the map below where the lightning might have
struck.

B •

A •

• C

D •

1 inch : 1 mile

6. In question 5, are there other places where the lightning could have
struck? _____ If so, show as many of those places as you can.

7. Lightning struck again! The person at point A heard the thunder 5 seconds after she saw the lightning. Show as many points as you can where the lightning could have struck.

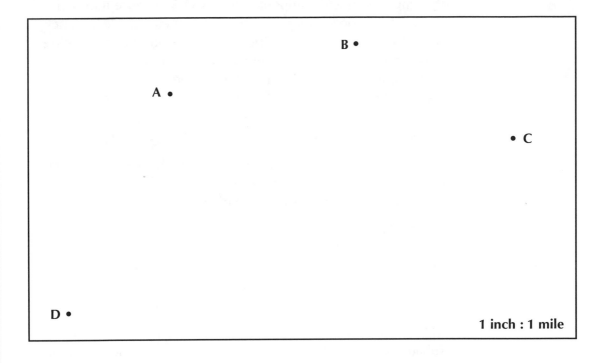

1 inch : 1 mile

8. The person at point C heard the thunder from that <u>same</u> lightning bolt 15 seconds after the lightning struck. Show where the lightning could have struck.

Rationale for the mathematics education community

This task involves geometry, measurement (direct and indirect), and arithmetic (particularly an application of division) in a non-standard, but interesting real-life setting. Proportional thinking is a critically important to this task because it provides the link between the map and the real-life setting. Each branch of mathematics is intertwined with the others in deriving answers to the task. The geometric part allows for multiple answers, including an entire line (or, more realistically, a segment). Although the immediate relevance of lightning depends somewhat on what part of the country one happens to live in, the phenomenon of nature will be familiar to all students.

As in several other examples in this collection, the choice of tools to use in attacking the problem is left up to each student. An array of tools should be made readily available.

The task also exemplifies the NCTM *Standards* because it includes questions that approach the problem setting from two directions. For example, question 3 asks for a distance, given a time, and question 4 asks for a time, given a distance. (In both instances, the distance must actually be measured on the map.)

Task design considerations: There are a number of fairly subtle points that should be mentioned in connection with the design of this task. It might be tempting to make this map less "abstract" by drawing little pictures of people on it rather than using the labeled dots. Unfortunately, that might make the map even more abstract. Suppose one draws a person about 1/8" high at D on a map whose scale is one inch for every mile. Then either the person at D is 600 feet tall or else the picture is merely a symbol for the person at D. A better alternative would be to use a "real" map — a road map, for instance — to make it less abstract.

One has to be very careful with tasks that involve quasi-real situations and be alert to students who may bring additional background information to the task. In this case, the task posits a situation in which an approximate rule of thumb is being used to make relatively rough calculations of distance. Depending on the air temperature, sound may travel at slightly different speeds, and, as a result, an answer to question 3 different from the expected one should be considered correct. (See the Protorubric section, below.)

Question 3 requires division of 12 by 5. The result, whether expressed as a decimal (2.4 inches) or as a fraction (2-2/5") does not correspond to the way most rulers are marked. The student must decide if the distance 2-9/16" or 2-3/8" is the better choice.

Notice that the distances are purposely made simpler in questions 7 and 8 than they were in question 3. The idea is not to confound the relatively difficult geometric ideas with numerical distractions.

Consider the wording of questions 5 and 6. Question 5, deliberately, makes no *a priori* judgments or assumptions about how many places the child will mark as a possible lightning sites. Question 6 is designed as a follow-up. If the child has already indicated the perpendicular bisector of segment AC for question 5, then the proper answer to question 6 is "no." On the other hand, there is nothing wrong with answering question 5 with a single point equidistant from A and C, and in that case, the proper answer to question 6 is "yes," followed by a description of the perpendicular bisector. If, instead, question 6 were worded as "In question 5, where else could lightning have struck? Show as many places as you can," then the student who has already given a full answer to question 5 is stuck.

Variants and extensions: Changing the numbers and placement of the dots for A, B, C, D, and the lightning, and consequently altering the difficulty of the task, create immediate variants. For example, the 12 seconds can be changed to 15, which would eliminate the need for fractional numbers of miles. Or the differences in distances could be made more obvious (although one would then be assessing less sophisticated measuring skills).

Standard English units of measure were used here, but metric units could just as well have been used. Metric units would make some of the calculations more straightforward.

Protorubric

Characteristics of the high response:

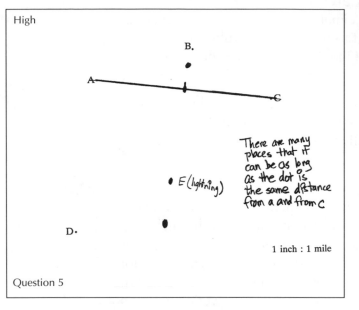

High

B.

A————————————C

E (lightning)

There are many places that it can be as long as the dot is the same distance from a and from c

D.

1 inch : 1 mile

Question 5

The high-level response shows that the student is making a fluent translation between the map and reality, thus demonstrating proportional reasoning. All the questions are answered satisfactorily. (Note that there may be some justification for saying that the person at D would hear the sound after 12 seconds if one uses a speed of sound different from the one implied by the rule of thumb. (See point 2 under Task design considerations, above.) If an adequate justification is provided, another answer to question 3 could be acceptable here.)

At the highest level, the perpendicular bisector of segment AC is described as the possible location for the lightning strike in question 6, although use of the geometric term is not necessary. A circle of radius 1″ is drawn around point A for question 7. For question 8, the intersection points of two circles are identified as the possible spots for the last lightning bolt.

At a somewhat lower level, more than one possible location, but not all of them, are drawn for these questions.

Drawing tools (ruler, compass, etc.) are chosen and used appropriately.

Characteristics of the medium response:

The response demonstrates that the map and its scale are generally well understood. The principal difference between the high and medium response is that the latter does not consider many possible locations for the lightning strikes. One point equidistant from A and C is found for question 5, but the answer to question 6 is "no."

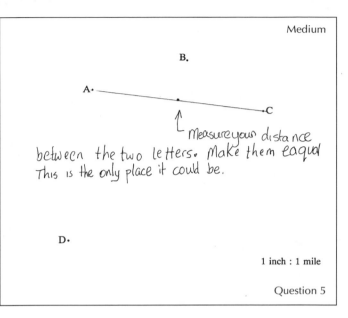

Characteristics of the low response:

The low response is characterized by thinking that is limited to one point or one distance at a time. Thus, while question 1 through 4 may be answered satisfactorily (although with limited justifications), no points that are equidistant from A and C are found.

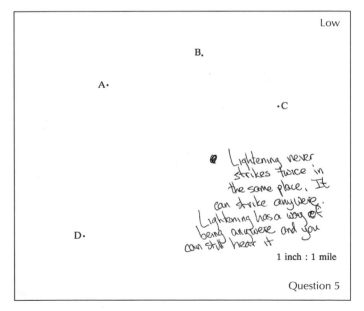

Comparing Grizzly Bears and Black Bears

Suggested time allotment
One class period

Student social organization
Students working alone or in pairs

Task

Assumed background: This item assumes that children have had extensive experience with analyzing sets of data, and, especially, with drawing the type of graph sometimes called a line plot. Students should be accustomed to deciding what kinds of analytic approaches to take. That is, their background

should go beyond creating graphs and computing averages to include making decisions about what kinds of computations or visual representations are appropriate in a given situation.

Presenting the task: The teacher should provide a short introduction to the subject matter of the assessment task — two kinds of bears that live in the Rocky Mountains of Montana. Rangers and biologists sometimes collect data on samples of bears. The task is to analyze two lists of data from individual grizzly bears and black bears.

As always, pencils, rulers, graph paper, calculators, etc., should be available.

Student assessment activity: See the following pages.

Name _____ **Date** _____

The data below give the weights of some grizzly bears and black bears living in the Rocky Mountains in Montana.

Grizzly bears			Black bears		
Bob	Male	220 lbs.	Blackberry	Female	230 lbs.
Rocky	Male	170 lbs.	Greta	Female	150 lbs.
Sue	Female	210 lbs.	Freddie	Male	140 lbs.
Linda	Female	330 lbs.	Harry	Male	230 lbs.
Wilma	Female	190 lbs.	Ken	Male	170 lbs.
Ed	Male	180 lbs.	Hilda	Female	220 lbs.
Glenda	Female	290 lbs.	Grumpy	Male	160 lbs.
Bill	Male	230 lbs.	Blackfoot	Female	150 lbs.
			Marcy	Female	170 lbs.
			Grempod	Male	200 lbs.

1. Organize these data in a way that would help you find which kind of bear is heavier — grizzly bears or black bears. (You can use another piece of paper to do this. Please be sure to put your name on it!)

2. Write down three things that you can tell about the weights of the bears. (You may want to use your answer from question 1 to help you.)

3. Based on these data, how much heavier is a typical bear of one kind than a typical bear of the other kind? _____

How did you figure out your answer?

Rationale for the mathematics education community

The task requires students to analyze a fairly complex set of measurements obtained from a "real world" context that is appealing to children of this age group. Rather than simply reading individual values on a graph or from a table, they must view the data set as a whole. More specifically, the problem reveals students' ability to create a representation that shows these data on a reasonable scale in a way that allows comparison of the two groups. (Some students may also find ways to show males and females within each group, thereby coping with one numerical and two categorical variables.)

A second reason for including the task in this collection is that it pushes the curriculum to include work in data analysis, specifically:

- organizing unordered data in a representation that reveals the overall shape and characteristics of the data set;

- describing data sets;

- summarizing data in a way that enables one to compare two data sets.

As with the other tasks in the collection, it requires students to communicate their thinking verbally and graphically.

Task design considerations: Note that there are not the same number of bears of each type, which forces the student to consider more than just the total weights. In fact, the data have been adjusted so that the sums of the weights are the same. This will serve as a subtle hint to the child who adds the two columns of figures and is tempted to stop at that point.

The heaviest bear in the entire set is a grizzly, which is the heaviest kind of bear. When looking at student responses, one must be careful to distinguish reasoning that relies on the difference between the central values of the weights from reasoning that simply cites the heaviest bear.

Even though many of the difficulties associated with performing computations on data have been obviated by the advent of inexpensive hand-held calculators, finding suitable "real world" data is still tricky. Of course children should have many opportunities to collect their own data, but occasionally one will have to create plausible data from scratch. (Actually, zookeepers and forest rangers do not often weigh adult bears because of the danger involved.) The data in this task come partly from the University of Montana's Office of Grizzly Bear Recovery, supplemented by additional reasonable weights.

Variants and extensions: Other kinds of questions can be asked about the data that are provided here: for example, "What can you say about the weights of male and female bears?" A deeper kind of question deals with age: "Do you think that all these bears are the same age? Explain why you think so."

Going beyond this set of data on bears, there are innumerable sources that can be used in creating data-analysis tasks — animal sizes, building heights, river lengths, and so forth. One must be careful, however, to be sure that whatever the objects are, they are equally familiar (or unfamiliar) to the students who are being assessed.

The teacher should be encouraged to follow up the assessment task with appropriate activities. In this case, one might want children to organize oral or written reports to the class using information about the other kinds of bears, perhaps illustrated with graphic displays, posters, etc.

Protorubric

This protorubric is based on the assumption that the child will interpret the task as one calling for the creation of some sort of graph.

Characteristics of the high response:

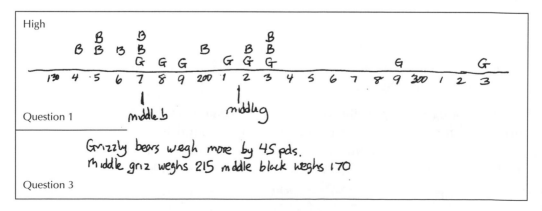

The graph represents the data clearly and accurately, with the scale and intervals chosen appropriately.

The description of the grizzly bears and black bears includes accurate observations about the ranges of the two sets of data and the way each set of data is distributed over its range (that is, some comments about center and spread, although these may not be in formal statistical terms).

The general conclusion reached is that grizzly bears are generally heavier than blacks, but some blacks weigh more than some grizzlies.

A number or range is chosen that represents the difference between the central values or central clumps of the two sets of data. A median, mean, or less formal measure of center is used (e.g., "Most of the grizzly bears clump around 200 pounds even though there are a few bigger ones and a few smaller ones, so I said that a typical grizzly bear is 200 . . . ").

Characteristics of the medium response:

The scale or intervals chosen are not chosen so as to show the data as clearly as possible, or there are a few inaccuracies in plotting the data.

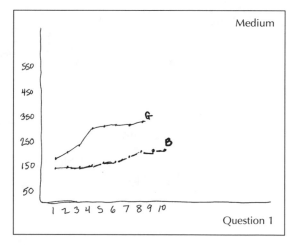

The description of the blacks and grizzlies does not include some of the important aspects about the range and center of the data.

The general conclusion reached could be interpreted to mean that all grizzlies weigh more than all blacks (that is, the overlap of the data is not noted).

A reasonable answer is given (that a typical grizzly bear weigh about 30 to 50 pounds more than a typical black bear) but the explanation is inadequate.

Characteristics of the low response:

The graph has major flaws that significantly impede comparisons of the two kinds of bears — for example, incorrectly plotted data, mislabeled axes, or inadequate distinction between the two types of bears.

The description of the data focuses on individual values rather than capturing features of the whole data set.

Either the wrong kind of bear is identified as the heavier one, or no reference is made to the graph at all in support of the conclusion. No attempt is made to consider the "typical" bear of either type; for example, two specific bears are chosen and the difference of their weights reported.

References

The "Used Numbers: Real Data in the Classroom" project at TERC.

The Towers Problem

Suggested time allotment
One class period

Student social organization
Small group work followed
by individual work

Task

*Use manipulatives in
problem solving*

*Apply exhaustive thinking to
create a convincing argument*

*Communicate results to others,
including work in small groups*

Assumed background:
This task requires children
to enumerate in some systematic fashion all possible ways of
constructing towers of blocks under certain constraints, and
then to explain convincingly that all the possibilities have been
found. Hence the task assumes that children have had prior
experiences with combinatorial situations, as well as with
explaining clearly how one can be sure that all the possibilities
have been determined.

Presenting the task: Initially the class is to work in groups of three. Each group should have a supply of Unifix® cubes of two different colors — about 40 cubes of each color. The teacher should explain that the task is to build towers of Unifix® cubes, saying something like this:

"Each tower is to be three cubes tall. You may use the cubes on your table, which include cubes of two different colors. Please build as many different towers as possible.

"Besides building the towers, please explain your work to the other students at your table, to convince them that you have not left any out, and that you have no duplicates. Please make only towers that are right-side up, like this:

and do not make any "upside down" towers, like this:

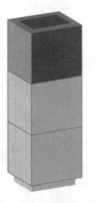

Then the teacher should pass out copies of the student sheet and read through the directions to be sure that everyone understands the task.

Student assessment activity: See the next page.

Name _____ **Date** _____

1. Please send a letter to a student who is ill and unable to come to school. Describe all of the different towers that you have built that are three cubes tall, when you had two colors available to work with. Why were you sure that you had made every possible tower and had not left any out?

Rationale for the mathematics education community

Problems or situations that involve systematic counting of the number of ways that something can be done provide good opportunities to students for problem solving, reasoning, and communicating their results to others. Although such problems from discrete mathematics are not explicitly called for in the K-4 *Standards*, they are described in the standards for the upper grades. The foundation for discrete mathematics can be laid early, particularly through the use of manipulatives.

An analysis of videotapes of the pilot tests on this task suggested that fourth graders' oral explanations in small groups often were much more detailed and sophisticated than their written explanations. That is, the "letters" that they write to their sick classmates often do not capture their full insight into the task. One would expect the discrepancy between written and oral explanations to diminish as students get more experience with the kinds of mathematical communication emphasized in the *Standards*.

The discrepancy may arise partly because the students know that their small-group colleagues will not accept inexact or unclear oral explanations, whereas a written letter provides no immediate feedback. This lack must be addressed, however, because the development of students' communication skills is an important goal of reform.

Task design considerations: This is an excellent task to illustrate the importance of the precise wording of questions. It is tempting to say "using two colors" instead of "when you had two colors available to work with." But some children will (correctly) interpret "using two colors" to mean that both colors must be used in each tower, and conclude that there are only six 3-block towers that use *exactly two* colors. There's certainly nothing wrong with the task of determining the number of towers that use exactly two colors, but it is not the same as the task of finding the number of towers that use *no more than two* colors. The essential point here is that small changes in the wording of questions can have significant and often unintended consequences. Ordinarily, it is not the aim of the task to have children make these subtle distinctions, so it is important for the task-writer to be sensitive to the differences that the wording can make.

The instructions deliberately say "Please send a letter to a student . . . ." instead of "Please write a letter to a student . . . ." Drawing pictures or tables or charts is a perfectly fine way to communicate results in this case; the aim is to avoid giving the impression that only "writing" is acceptable. For the same reason there are no lines on which to write — just blank space that the student can use as he or she wants to.

The directions for the teacher specify that Unifix® cubes be used. Other kinds of colored cubes are often used in elementary school classrooms, but one should be aware that certain brands of cubes can snap together on their sides, so that L-shaped towers can be built. As a result, these cubes are not appropriate for this task unless the students understand that only three-in-a-row towers are to be counted.

Variants and extensions: This task lends itself well to simple alterations of the numbers: One can change the height of the towers or the number of different colors that are available. Moreover, one can vary the difficulty of the task by changing the rules that determine what towers are allowable. For example, how many towers five blocks high can be made from red or blue blocks if no pair of blue blocks can touch each other?

One can vary the whole context as well, using something other than towers of blocks. Care must be taken to ensure that the mathematics of the situation is still what is intended. Consider, for instance, the problem of creating rows of plants in a garden. Blue-flowered plants and red-flowered plants are available. How many different rows of three plants are possible? This is not the same as the towers problem because a garden row can be viewed from either side; R-R-B is the same as B-R-R.

Protorubric

Characteristics of the high response:

High

To a Person,

I knew how many their are because 1=2 2=4 3=8 4=16 5=32, and on. Start with)

| R | | M | ←

Then you can only make two 1 block towers.

| R | | W | R | | W |
| R | | R | W | | W |

you can only make four 2 towers. soon you will see a pattern

R	W	R	W	R	W	R	W
R	W	W	R	R	W	W	W
R	R	R	R	W	W	W	W

Their all different — is all of the ways.

Question 1

The high response shows recognition of the need for a systematic scheme to keep track of "all possibilities" in a way that supports a conclusion that there could not be any other towers of height three. The student reasoning does not rely on the argument that "I cannot think of any others," but instead presents some reasonable scheme that is potentially exhaustive.

Among the arguments that children invented in the pilot are these three:

Proof by cases. There is only one tower that has zero blues. There are three towers with exactly one blue (in the bottom, middle, or top positions in the tower). There are three towers with exactly two blues (there is usually some weakness in the argument at this point). And there is one tower with three blues. Total: 8 different towers.

Improved proof by cases. Same as above, but the troublesome "exactly two blues" is handled by arguing that two blues implies exactly one red, which is easy to keep track of: bottom, middle, or top.

Proof by induction. There are four different towers that are two cubes tall — BB, BR, RB, and RR. Atop each of these can go either a blue or a red. The resulting towers are all different because they differ either in their top color or in the color of one of the lower blocks.

Characteristics of the medium response:

The response shows some suggestion of a method for being exhaustive, but shows no recognition that this feature is present or that it is needed.

There may also be explicit statements to the effect that "I couldn't find any more."

An answer qualifies as medium if it presents a proof of some important part of the problem — for example, that the number of towers must be even because every tower has exactly one "opposite" by interchanging the colors.

Medium

Dear Ronald Mcdonald
You missed a great Day of math. Amy came and we worked with unifix cubes. We had to make towers with 3 cubes. Here's how they looked W stands for white and M stands for Maron

I moved maroon up until it got to the top then I did the same thing but I used white. The other 2 are all white and all maroon.

Question 1

Characteristics of the low response:

Low

Dear Dyshon
my Solution is that their are eight (8) towers in all. I will draw you the cubes I have made =
I am sure because when I tried to make more of them and to compare them it was still the same.

Question 1

The letter describes one or more methods for generating new towers, but fails to deal with the question of devising a method that will exhaustively produce all possible towers, and shows no recognition of the need for such a method.

The Hog Game

Suggested time allotment
A total of two or three class periods

Student social organization
Students working in pairs

Task

Assumed background: This task uses a game called Hog to pose questions that require students to use two areas of mathematics to answer. On the first day the questions concern combinatorics and reasoning about the possibility or impossibility of certain outcomes. On the second day the questions concern strategies for playing the game, based on the probabilities involved. Therefore, students should have had experience with both areas: They should be familiar with analyzing situations by enumerating all the possibilities; and they should have had experience with probabilistic situations (games in particular) that are more complex than simple coin-tossing and that require the collection

of data. The idea of formulating and communicating a strategy for playing a game should be familiar to them.

Presenting the task: The teacher should pass out the first student sheet and several number cubes (cubes numbered from 1 to 6) to each pair of students being assessed. The teacher should then read through the directions for the game and the three examples to be sure that everyone has an understanding of the rules of the game. Students should then be given the opportunity to play the game to see how it works.

Doing Part 1 (Questions 1 through 4) will be the first class period, and Part 2 (Questions 5 and 6) can be done in another one or two periods. Students should be given as much time as they need to gather a considerable amount of data as they respond to Questions 5 and 6.

Student assessment activity: See the following pages.

This is a game called HOG. You will need number cubes, a cup, and pencil and paper. The object of the game is to get as large a score as you can.

Here are the rules:

1. Say how many number cubes you want to put in the cup.

2. Roll that many number cubes from the cup.

3. If <u>none</u> of the numbers you rolled is a 1, then your score is the <u>sum</u> of the numbers you rolled.

4. If a 1 comes up on <u>any</u> of your number cubes, then your score is 0.

Here are some examples:

Example: Mary said that she wanted to put 3 number cubes in the cup. Here's what she got: Since she didn't get any 1's, her score is 5 + 2 + 4, or 11.

Example: Justina said that she wanted to put 7 number cubes in the cup. Here's what she got: Since she got a 1 (in fact, she got two of them), her score is 0.

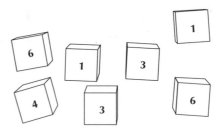

Example: José said that he wanted to put 3 number cubes in the cup. The numbers he rolled were: 5, 6, and 1. His score was 0.

You and your partner should play the game for a while to see how it works. Then answer these questions:

Part 1

1. Tsao-lim said he wanted put 8 number cubes in the cup. He got 3, 5, 1, 4, 4, 4, 6, and 2.

   What was his score? _____ Why?

2. Jeffella said she wanted to put 8 number cubes in the cup. She got 3, 5, 2, 4, 4, 4, 6, and 2.

   What was her score? _____ Why?

3. Karl put 2 number cubes in the cup. His score was 7. List all of the ways he could have gotten a 7 with 2 number cubes.

4. Johann said he wanted to put 8 number cubes in the cup. It turned out that his score was 19.

    a. Could all of the number cubes have been 3s? _____
       Explain why or why not.

    b. Could 3 of the 8 number cubes have been 3s? _____
       Explain why or why not.

    c. Could one of the number cubes have been a 6? _____
       Explain why or why not.

Here are some more questions about the game called HOG. Remember, the object of the game is to get as large a score as you can. Also, if any number cube you roll is a 1, then your score is 0.

Part 2

5. Estrella found a very large cup and said she wanted to put 100 number cubes in it. What do you think her score would probably be? _____ Explain why you think so.

6. Roberto says he has a <u>strategy</u> for playing HOG. His strategy is to put 2 number cubes in the cup every time he plays.

Quentin says he has a different strategy for playing HOG. Quentin's strategy is to put 1 number cube in the cup every time he plays.

One partner should play HOG for a while using Roberto's strategy, and the other partner should play the game for a while using Quentin's strategy. Keep track of what happens.

Which strategy do you think is better — Roberto's or Quentin's? _____ Explain your answer.

7. Suppose you want to find the best strategy for playing HOG. Each time you play it, you're going to use the <u>same number of cubes</u> in the cup. Remember that you are trying to get the highest total score for whatever number of times you play. How many number cubes would you choose to put in the cup? _____ Please explain how you decided on this number.

8. How sure are you that you have found the best strategy? Why do you think that?

Rationale for the mathematics education community

The Hog Game, as noted earlier, illustrates how the same underlying situation can be used as a vehicle for exploring different areas of mathematics. In this case, some of the questions about the game involve relatively simple numerical concepts, while other questions involve more sophisticated ideas from probability. Even the simplest numerical questions are non-routine, however, and are presented in a format that requires the child to explain his or her reasoning carefully.

Even though the rules of the game are straightforward (and in fact will already be familiar to some children), optimal strategies are not at all obvious. That is, students will not come to the Hog Game task with an *a priori* idea of what is "supposed" to happen. (In contrast, tasks that are based on activities like flipping a fair coin and counting heads or tails often do not promote genuine exploration, and may even discourage it because children have preconceptions about what the results "should" turn out to be.)

This prototype is also another good example of an assessment task that can be linked back into instruction, through a whole-class discussion of results. One possibility is to pool the results obtained in responding to question 6, to get a more definitive idea of what strategies work best. Another is to take advantage of the computer technology that is widely available in U.S. classrooms to create a simulation of the Hog game. A very simple computer program, written in BASIC appears in an appendix to this task. (No amount of simulated play is going to be able to distinguish the strategy of putting 5 number cubes in the cup from the strategy of using 6 number cubes, because the two strategies both yield an expected score of 8, which is the best score that can be obtained. One run of a computer simulation yielded mean scores of 8.008 and 8.067 for 5 and 6 number cubes, respectively, with each strategy being used in 200,000 games.)

Task design considerations: Some students today play a game similar to this one that is known as PIG. Usually the rules state that the player declares how many times he or she is going to roll a single number cube; if the number cube shows 1 on any roll then the player's score is 0; otherwise it is the sum of the rolls. The rules are easier to convey, however, if they are phrased in terms of rolling, once, a cup containing a pre-determined number of cubes. Unfortunately for the sake of classroom logistics, the many-cubes-in-the-cup version requires a larger supply of number cubes if all the children are going to be engaged in the task simultaneously. One way of handling this is to have only a few pairs of children working on the task at the same time.

The point of making Tsao-lim's and Jeffella's rolls in questions 1 and 2 identical — except that Jeffella got a 2 instead of Tsao-lim's 1 — is to reinforce the difference that a single number cube can make. Tsao-lim's and Jeffella's scores are not just 1 apart; Tsao-lim's 1 makes his score 0.

Note that the instructions just before the first question (as well as in questions 5 and 6) are very directive: playing the game is not left as an option. On the other hand, one of the decisions that is left up to each pair of students is how many times they should play in answering questions 5 and 6 — that is, how much data they should gather. Ultimately, of course, one would want students to view playing the game as just another tool that can be used or not used in approaching a problem, and one would want to assess the degree to which children use that tool, if it is appropriate, on their own, without explicit directions to do so.

Similarly, the instruction to "Keep track of what happens" in question 6 is deliberately vague; the students are given no guidance about how to organize their results.

Question 8 was added after the first round of pilot testing, in an attempt to tap the level of confidence that the student has in his or her results. Ideally, the student should be able to distinguish the certainty of a response to question 4c (it is impossible for Johann to get a score of 19 with 8 number cubes if one of them is a 6) from the tentative nature of a response based on a limited number of trials.

Variants and extensions:

Part 1. There are many variants of the simple numerical questions that can be posed along the lines suggested in question 4. A more substantial variant is to ask how many number cubes a player who gets a certain score might have been using. For example, if Johann got a score of 19, what is the largest number of cubes he might have been using? What is the smallest number of cubes that he might have used? Or: Emmy rolls twice, using the same number of cubes each time. First she gets a score of 11, and then she gets a score of 23. How many cubes are in her cup?

Part 2. This task provides a good example of how the inclusion of intermediate questions can provide a "scaffolding" to help students approach the problem of deciding whether Roberto's or Quentin's strategy is better. For example, after Roberto's and Quentin's strategies are described, one might ask:

> When Roberto rolls the two number cubes, what numbers could he get? List all the possible rolls with two number cubes. Then, for each one, write the score that Roberto would get for that roll. (One might even provide a 6-by-6 table to be filled out with the scores that Roberto could obtain.) Now do the same for Quentin: List all the possible rolls he could get with one number cube, and for each one write his score. Based on your findings, which strategy do you think is better — Roberto's or Quentin's? Explain your answer.

By *not* providing the additional questions suggested above, the task becomes more open-ended because it requires the child to supply the analytic tools (e.g. a 6-by-6 table of possible outcomes for two number cubes) that are needed.

Question 7 structures the strategy-finding task by specifying that the cup must contain the same number of cubes on every roll. An alternative would be to relax that condition. In a less structured version of the task, one child said that she would start with one cube, and increase that by one cube on every roll until she got a score of zero. Then on the next roll she would remove one cube (unless there were only one cube in the cup). This is the sort of variant that could be explored after the assessment is finished.

Protorubric

The fact that the Hog Game assessment task is divided into two parts, involving different mathematical ideas and to be done on different days, highlights the issue of the scope of the scoring rubric. Essentially there are two options in this instance: to treat the two parts separately, with a scoring rubric for each, or to lump them together under a single scoring rubric. The second alternative simply exacerbates the problem of making unambiguous judgments, since it is possible that many children will do better on one part of the task than on the other. Hence two protorubrics are provided below, one for each component of the task.

Part 1

Characteristics of the high response:

The responses to questions 1 and 2 are correct (0 and 30, respectively) with justifications that assert that (a) Tsao-Lim got a 1, and so his score is 0; and (b) Jeffella did not get any 1s, and so her score is the sum of the numbers showing.

> High
>
> No—
> Because that leaves 13 left and you'd have to make the rest twos in order to get 8 cubes. Seven cubes would give 14. There would be too many two's in order to get only 19 and be 8 cubes.
>
> Question 4c (Part 1)

In question 3, the pairs 5 and 2, and 4 and 3 are listed. (Listing the pairs 2 and 5, and 3 and 4 as well is perfectly acceptable, but not necessary, since the context does not require 2 and 5 to be considered as being different from 5 and 2.)

The answers to questions 4a, b, and c are correct (No, Yes, and No, respectively), and the justifications are clear and accurate. In question 4c, for instance, the justification amounts to the following argument: Since his score was 19, he didn't get any 1's. But if one of his rolls had been a 6, then even if all of Johann's other rolls were 2's, his score would be at least 20. So he couldn't have had a 6.

Characteristics of the medium response:

The justifications given for the answers to questions 1 and 2 are not completely accurate, even though the scores given are correct.

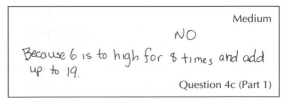

> Medium
>
> NO
> Because 6 is to high for 8 times and add up to 19.
>
> Question 4c (Part 1)

The pair 1 and 6 is given as a possibility in question 3, forgetting that the 1 would result in a score of 0.

The reasons cited for one or more of questions 4a, b, and c are not complete. For example, the response to 4c is something like: No, because 6 would be too big.

Characteristics of the low response:

> Low
>
> Because there could be 5 yes
> 2's an one 3
>
> Question 4c (Part 1)

There is evidence in questions 1 and 2 that the student forgets or ignores the fundamental rule of the Hog Game. As an example, the answer to question 1 might be 29 (the sum of the rolls, forgetting that the 1 makes the score zero).

In question 2, there is a mistake in the arithmetic by at most 1, resulting in a score of 29 or 31.

In question 3, numbers may be offered that are not even on the number cubes (e.g., 0 and 7).

The responses to questions 4a, b, and c show pervasive misunderstandings. For example, the response to 4a might be: Yes, because 8 X 3 = 24.

Part 2

Characteristics of the high response:

> High
>
> Normally Quentin's because you have a greater chance of NOT getting a one. But only once out of 10 games we rolled a 1 with Quentins and we rolled one 3 times out of 10 games with Roberto's so Roberto's gave the most score.
>
> Question 6 (Part 2)

The student says that Estrella's score would probably be 0, because it is very likely that at least one of the 100 number cubes will show a 1. (If her score *isn't* 0, it could be anything from 200 to 600, but that information is *not* required.)

One highest-level response to question 6 is an analysis that shows all of Roberto's possible outcomes in a 6-by-6 table. The sum of the scores of the 36 equally likely games is 200, and hence the average score per game using Roberto's strategy is 200/36. Quentin's strategy, on the other hand, allows 6 possible games, all equally likely; the average score is 20/6. Hence Roberto's strategy is better.

A somewhat lower-level response (but perfectly satisfactory for this age level) would be to play the game perhaps 20 times with each strategy, and then compute an average score for each.

On the low end of the high category is the response that Quentin's strategy is better because Roberto has a greater chance of throwing a 1, and therefore a better chance of getting a score of 0.

For question 7, the response should describe a process of trying various candidates for the number of cubes to put in the cup. The student should take into account the results obtained so far — that is, that rolling two cubes is better than rolling only one, and that rolling 100 cubes is not good. One good approach to finding an optimal number is one of successive approximation: Try putting 10 cubes in the cup and see what happens. Then try 5 cubes, etc.

For each candidate strategy, the students should play about 20 (or more) trial games, computing an average score for each. The final strategy chosen should be based on the empirical evidence gathered. No fourth-grade child should be expected to choose a strategy on any basis more sophisticated than the successive approximation method outlined above. (The best strategy is to put either 5 or 6 number cubes in the cup.)

The response to question 8 should admit a degree of uncertainty that is appropriate for the strategy chosen and the justification provided. If the successive approximation technique is used, the high-level response would be something like: "I'm not very sure that this is the best strategy. Maybe if I tried it lots more times I would find that some other number of cubes would be better to put in the cup."

Characteristics of the medium response:

Question 7 (Part 2)

In general, either the explanations are incomplete or else there is some partial forgetting of the rules of the game. In question 5, for instance, the response is 0, with no explanation, or something around 300 or 400, with an explanation that claims there are 100 rolls and each one is going to be around a 3 or a 4.

In question 6, the response is empirically based on playing the game repeatedly, but using a small number of trials, or based on trials that are not clearly organized. Or the claim is that Roberto's strategy is better because he rolls more and hence has more of a chance to get more points (i.e., not taking into account that Roberto also has a bigger chance of rolling a 1, and thus getting a score of 0).

The answer to question 7 is based on a limited number of trials with just a few different numbers of cubes in the cup. A conclusion of "put 5 cubes in the cup", for example, might be reached without an explicit exploration of 4 and 6 cubes.

Characteristics of the low response:

Question 7 (Part 2)

Question 8 (Part 2)

The responses to questions 6 and 7 are not at all based on any systematic, empirical investigation of the situation. Instead, the child plays the game just a few times (if at all) and records results in a way that does not convey any sense of keeping track of what is happening. The student leaps to a conclusion about Roberto and Quentin (or about optimal strategies in general) without justification, even though he or she may give the "correct answer" that Roberto's strategy is better.

Even an accurate answer to question 8 (such as: "I'm not sure I found the best strategy, because all I did was to guess") would not lift the response out of the low category.

Appendix

The following is a program written in Applesoft BASIC to simulate the playing of HOG. It calls for the number of number cubes to be put in the cup and for the number of rolls to be made. It then prints out the average score obtained.

```
10      INPUT "HOW MANY NUMBER CUBES DO YOU
        WANT TO PUT IN THE CUP? "; D
20      INPUT "HOW MANY GAMES DO YOU WANT TO
        PLAY? "; G
30      T = 0: REM THIS COUNTS TOTAL SCORE
40      FOR I = 1 TO G
50      S = 0: REM THIS IS THE SCORE WITHIN A SINGLE
        GAME
60      FOR J = 1 TO D: REM LOOK AT EACH CUBE
70      R = INT(6 * RND(1))+1: REM THIS IS A RANDOM
        WHOLE NUMBER BETWEEN 1 AND 6
80      IF R = 1 THEN GOTO 200: REM THE PROCESS IS
        SHORT-CIRCUITED AS SOON AS A 1 APPEARS
90      S = S + R: REM THE CUBE ISN'T 1, SO ADD IT TO
        THE SCORE
100     NEXT J
110     T = T + S
120     NEXT I
130     PRINT "THE AVERAGE SCORE, PLAYING ";G;"
        GAMES, WITH ";D;" NUMBER CUBES, WAS ";T/G;"."
140     PRINT: PRINT "DO YOU WANT TO PLAY AGAIN?
        (Y/N)"
150     GET Q$
160     IF Q$ = "Y" THEN GOTO 10
170     END
200     S = 0: J = D: GOTO 100
```

Resources

Publications

California Assessment Program (1989). *A question of thinking: A first look at students' performance on open-ended questions in mathematics.* Sacramento: California State Department of Education.

Mathematical Sciences Education Board (1990). *Reshaping school mathematics: A philosophy and framework for curriculum.* Washington: National Academy Press.

——, (1991). *Counting on you: Actions supporting mathematics teaching standards.* Washington: National Academy Press.

——, (undated). *For good measure: Principles and goals for mathematics assessment.* Washington: National Academy Press.

National Commission on Excellence in Education (1983). *A nation at risk: The imperative for educational reform.* Washington: U.S. Government Printing Office.

National Council of Teachers of Mathematics (1989). *Curriculum and evaluation standards for school mathematics.* Reston (VA): Author.

——, (1991). *Professional standards for teaching mathematics.* Reston, (VA): Author.

National Research Council (1989). *Everybody counts: A report to the nation on the future of mathematics education.* Washington: National Academy Press.

Pandey, Tej (1991). *A sampler of mathematics assessment.* Sacramento: California Department of Education.

Steen, Lynn Arthur (ed.) (1990). *On the shoulders of giants: New approaches to numeracy.* Washington: National Academy Press.

Stenmark, J. K. (1989). *Assessment alternatives in mathematics: An overview of assessment techniques that promote learning.* Berkeley: University of California.

___ (ed.), (1991). *Mathematics assessment: Myths, models, good questions, and practical suggestions.* Reston (VA): NCTM.

U.S. Department of Education (1991). *America 2000: An education strategy.* Washington: Author.

State Coalitions

Alabama Coalition for Mathematics Education, Barbara S. Rice, 205/851-5316, Dept. of Mathematics, Alabama A & M University, PO Box 326, Normal, AL 35762

Council for Alaskan Mathematics and Science Education, Chris Birch, 907/265-8299, Alyeska Pipeline Service Company, 1835 Bragaw, Anchorage, AK 99512

Arizona Mathematics Coalition, Philip A. Leonard, 602/965-3792, Dept. of Mathematics, Arizona State University, Tempe, AZ 85287-1804

Arkansas State Mathematics Coalition, William W. Durand, 501/246-5511, Dept. of Mathematics, Henderson State University, Box 7667, Arkadelphia, AR 71923

California Coalition for Mathematics, Kenneth C. Millett, 805/893-3894, Dept. of Mathematics, University of California, Santa Barbara, CA 93160

Colorado Alliance for Science Mathematics Council, Glenn Bruckhart, 303/795-6881, 1149 Ridge Road, Littleton, CO 80120

Connecticut Academy for Education in Mathematics, Science, and Technology, Richard C. Cole, 203/346-1177, The Connecticut Academy for Education in Mathematics, Science, and Technology, 178 Cross Street, Middleton, CT 06457

Delaware Mathematics Connections Coalition, Patricia L. Hirschy, 302/571-5328, Dept. of Mathematics, Deleware Technical Community College, 333 Shipley Street, Wilmington, DE 19801

District of Columbia Mathematics Coalition, Paula Duckett, 202/724-4589, River Terrace Community School, 34th and Dix Streets, NE, Washington, DC 20019

Florida Leadership Alliance for Improvement of Mathematics Education, Douglas K. Brumbaugh, 407/823-5866, College of Education, University of Central Florida, Orlando, FL 32816

Georgia Coalition for Excellence in Mathematics Education, David Stone, 912/681-5335, Dept. of Mathematics & Computer Science, Georgia Southern University, Landrum Box 8093, Statesboro, GA 30460

Hawaii State Mathematics Coalition, W. Gary Martin, 808/956-9956, Curriculum Research Development Group, 1776 University Avenue, Honolulu, HI 96822

Idaho Mathematics Coalition, Jerry Young, 208/385-3389, Dept. of Mathematics, Boise State University, 1910 University Drive, Boise, ID 83725

Illinois Mathematics Coalition, Anthony Peressini, 217/333-6336, Mathematics Dept., University of Illinois at Urbana-Champaign, 273 Altgeld Hall, 1409 West Green Street, Urbana, IL 61801

Indiana Mathematics, Science & Technology Education Alliance, G. William Anderson, 317/873-2858, Eagle Union Community School Corporation, 690 Beach Street, Zionsville, IN 46077

Iowa Mathematics Coalition, Larry P. Leutzinger, 319/273-2631, Dept. of Mathematics & Computer Science, University of Northern Iowa, Cedar Falls, IA 50614

Kansas Mathematical Sciences Education Coalition, Inc., William Richardson, 316/689-3160, Dept. of Mathematics and Statistics, The Witchita State University, Campus Box 33, Witchita, KS 67208

Kentucky Mathematics Coalition, William S. Bush, 606/257-2927, University of Kentucky, 335 Dickey Hall, Lexington, KY 40506-0017

Louisiana Mathematics Coalition, Jean Reddy Clement, 504/342-1136, Louisiana Dept. of Education, PO Box 99064, Baton Rouge, LA 70804-9064

Maine Mathematics Alliance, Francis Q. Eberle, 207/775-7362, STAR Foundation, 20 Danforth Street, Portland, ME 04101

Maryland Mathematics Coalition, William Moulds, 410/830-3247, Mathematics Dept., Towson State University, ST302, Towson, MD 21204-7097

Massachusetts Mathematics Initiative, William Masalski, 413/545-1577, School of Education, University of Massachusetts, Amherst, MA 01003

Michigan Mathematics Education Coalition, Charles R. Allan, 517/373-1024, Michigan Dept. of Education, Box 30008, Lansing, MI 48909

Minnesota Mathematics Mobilization (M^3), Harvey Keynes, 612/625-2861, University of Minnesota, 115 Benson Hall, Minneapolis, MN 55455

Mississippi Mathematics Coalition, John R. Gilbert, 601/325-7142, Mississippi State University, Drawer MA, Jackson, MS 39762

Coalition for Missouri Mathematics, Vena Long, 816/235-2444, School of Education, University of Missouri, 5100 Rockhill Road, Kansas City, MO 64110

Montana Mathematics Coalition, Lawrence Kaber, 406/756-5099, Montana Council of Teachers of Mathematics, Flathead County High School, 644 Fourth Ave West, Kalispell, MT 59901

Nebraska Mathematics & Science Coalition, Karen Ward, 402/472-8965, PO Box 880326, Lincoln, NE 68588-0326

Nevada State Mathematics Coalition Herb Steffens, 702/687-3187, 908 East Robinson, Carson City, NV 89701

New Hampshire Mathematics, Science, & Technology Coalition, Enid Burrows, 603/535-2307, Dept. of Mathematics, Plymouth State College, Hyde Hall, Plymouth, NH 03264

New Jersey Mathematics Coalition, Joseph G. Rosenstein, 908/932-4065, Rutgers University, PO Box 10867, New Brunswick, NJ 08906

New Mexico Mathematics Coalition, Susan Gardenhire, 505/293-0947, 10605 Moonvalley Court, NE, Albuquerque, NM 87111

New York State Mathematics Coalition, Howard C. Johnson, 315/443-2373, Syracuse University, 304 Tolley Administration Bldg., Syracuse, NY 13210

North Carolina Mathematics & Science Coalition, Susan Friel, 919/966-3256, University of North Carolina, 210 Peabody Hall, CB 3345, Chapel Hill, NC 27599-3345

North Dakota Mathematics Coalition, James Babb, 701/857-3075, Dept. of Mathematics and Computer Sciences, Minot State University, Minot, ND 58701

Ohio Mathematics Coalition, Richelle M. Blair, 614/466-6000, Project Discovery, 3600 State Office Tower, 30 East Broad Street, Columbus, OH 43266-0417

Coalition for the Advancement of Mathematics Education in Oklahoma (CAMEO), J. Brian Conrey, 405/744-5688, Dept. of Mathematics, Oklahoma State University, Stillwater, OK 74078

Oregon Mathematics Coalition, Wallace Rogelstad, 503/655-9490, The Math Learning Center, 7660 Cason Lane, Gladstone, OR 97027

Pennsylvania State Mathematics Coalition, Mary Ann Matras, 717/424-3440, Dept. of Mathematics, East Stroudsburg University, East Stroudsburg, PA 18301

Rhode Island Mathematical Sciences Education Coalition, Stephanie Sullivan, 401/455-4058, 201 Charles Street, Providence, RI 02904-2213

South Carolina Mathematics Coalition, John Luedeman, 803/656-5222, Mathematical Sciences and Education, Clemson University, Martin Hall, Clemson, SC 29634-1907

South Dakota Mathematics Coalition, John Paul Jewett, 605/428-5473, Dell Rapids School District, 1216 Garfiels, Dell Rapids, SD 57022-1036

Tennessee Mathematics Coalition, Henry Frandsen, 615/974-4302, Dept. of Mathematics, University of Tennessee, Knoxville, TN 37996-1300

Mathematics Education Board of Texas, Clarence Dockweiler 409/845-8396, Dept. of EDCI, Texas A & M University, College Station, TX 77843

Utah Math, Science and Technology Coalition, Hal G. Moore, 801/532-6284, 1200 Beneficial Life Tower, Salt Lake City, UT 84111

Vermont State Mathematics Coalition, John A. Devino, 802/658-1570, Colchester High School, Box 31 Laker Drive, Colchester, VT 05446

Virginia Mathematics Coalition, Reuben W. Farley, 804/367-1319, Dept. of Mathematical Sciences, Virginia Commonwealth University, 1015 W. Main Street, Richmond, VA 23284

Washington State Mathematics Coalition, Jack Beal, 206/543-6636, 19026 107th Place, NE, Bothell, WA 98011

West Virginia Mathematics Coalition, Elizabeth Frye, 304/367-4621, 22 Park Drive, Fairmont, WV 26554

Wisconsin CASE Mathematics Education Coalition, Arnold Chandler, 608/238-5582, 4429 Somerset Lane, Madison, WI 53711

Wyoming Mathematics Coalition, Terry Jenkins, 307/766-4222, Dept. of Mathematics, University of Wyoming, Laramie, WY 82701

Mathematical Sciences Education Board

David L. Crippens, Senior Vice President-Educational Enterprises, KCET-TV, PBS, Los Angeles, CA

Gilbert J. Cuevas, Professor, Department of Teaching & Learning, School of Education, University of Miami, Coral Gables, FL

Philip A. Daro*, Director, American Mathematics Project, University of California, Oakland, CA

Daniel T. Dolan, Associate Director, PIMMS Project, Wesleyan University, Middletown, CT

Sue T. Dolezal, Mathematics Instructor, Sentinel High School, Missoula, MT

Dale Ewen, Past-President, American Mathematical Association of Two-Year Colleges, and Vice President for Academic Services, Parkland College, Champaign, IL

Joseph A. Fernandez, Chancellor, New York City Board of Education, Brooklyn, NY

Gary Froelich, Mathematics Instructor, Bismarck High School, Bismarck, ND

John Gage, Director, Science Office, Sun Microsystems, Inc., Mountain View, CA

Ramesh A. Gangolli, Professor of Mathematics, University of Washington, Seattle, WA

Linda M. Gojak, Mathematics Department Chair (K-8), Hawken School, Lyndhurst, OH

Jackie Goldberg, Ulysses S. Grant High School, Van Nuys, CA

Jacqueline E. Goodloe, Elementary Mathematics Resource Teacher, Burrville Elementary School, Washington, DC

Ronald L. Graham (NAS), Adjunct Director, Research, Information Sciences Division, AT&T Bell Labs, and Professor of Mathematical Sciences, Rutgers University, New Brunswick, NJ

Patricia S. Henry, President, The National PTA, Lawton, OK

Norbert Hill, Executive Director, American Indian Science & Engineering Society, Boulder, CO

Elizabeth M. Jones, K-12 Mathematics Consultant, Lansing School District, Lansing, MI

James S. Kahn*, President and Director, Museum of Science and Industry, Chicago, IL

Harvey B. Keynes, Professor of Mathematics and Director, Special Projects, University of Minnesota, Minneapolis, MN

Sue Ann McGraw, Mathematics Instructor, Lake Oswego High School, Lake Oswego, OR

Ruth R. McMullin*, Acting President and Chief Executive Officer, Harvard Business School Publishing Group, Boston, MA

Fernando Oaxaca, President, Coronado Communications, Los Angeles, CA

Richard A. Tapia (NAE), Professor of Mathematical Sciences, Rice University, Houston, TX

Daniel J. Teague, Instructor of Mathematics, North Carolina School of Mathematics & Science, Durham, NC

John S. Toll, President, Universities Research Association, Washington, DC, and Chancellor Emeritus and Professor of Physics, University of Maryland, College Park, MD

Philip Uri Treisman, Department of Mathematics, University of Texas, Austin, TX

Larry DeVan Williams, Mathematics Instructor, Eastwood Middle School, Tuscaloosa, AL

James J. Wynne, Manager, Biology and Molecular Science, IBM T.J. Watson Research Center, Yorktown Heights, NY

Credits

ASSESSMENT PROTOTYPIC WRITING GROUP
Lowell Carmony, Lake Forest College
Robert Davis, Rutgers University
Susan Jo Russell, TERC
Joan Rutherford, Haynesbridge (GA) Public Schools
Lourdes Santiago, Boston Public Schools
Paul Shoecraft, University of Houston-Victoria

SCHOOLS COOPERATING IN PILOT TESTING
Bloomington Elementary School, Bloomington, TX
Comal Independent School District, New Braunfels, TX
Frazier Elementary School, New Braunfels, TX
Green Acres School, Rockville, MD
Harding Elementary School, Kenilworth, NJ
Lincoln Elementary School, New Brunswick, NJ
Madderra-Fournoy School, Beeville, TX
Mountain Valley Elementary, Canyon Lake, TX
Pleasant Ridge School, Glenview, IL

SOFTWARE DEVELOPMENT
David Mark, M/MAC, Arlington, VA

PHOTOGRAPHY
Introduction
    H. Armstrong Roberts, Inc.
    Fairfax County (VA) Public Schools
Prototypes
    Benjamin D. Lourie

SPANISH TRANSLATIONS
Lourdes Santiago, Boston Public Schools

NATIONAL ACADEMY PRESS
Linda Humphrey, Design and Composition
Carla McCullough, Production
Sally Stanfield, Editorial Coordination

MATHEMATICAL SCIENCES EDUCATION BOARD
Lynn A. Steen, Executive Director
Linda P. Rosen, Associate Executive Director
Edward Esty, Senior Project Director
Ramona Robertson, Senior Project Assistant
Maren K. Olsen, Project Assistant